WA

The life of soaring legend Wally Scott

by Samantha Hilbert Thomas

WA – the life of soaring legend Wally Scott.

Copyright © 2010 by Samantha Hilbert Thomas

Published by BTLink Publishing,

P.O. Box 434, Big Flats, NY 14814

Excerpts of articles reprinted courtesy
of the Soaring Society of America.

Cover design by Just Ink. Front cover photograph courtesy National Soaring Museum.

ISBN 978-0-9831306-0-4

Printed in the United States of America

For Boots…forever plus two days

Wallace A. Scott. Marfa, TX 1970

CONTENTS

Foreword

When I stopped by Al Parker's soaring school at Odessa, Texas in the summer of 1962 to sample West Texas soaring, I did not imagine that it would be the beginning of a series of summers that would become the most enjoyable part of my soaring career. The hospitality of Wallace and Boots Scott, Red Wright and Al Parker, combined with the West Texas soaring weather, soon made it apparent that this would not be a one-time visit.

The following summer found me back in Odessa with a Schleicher Ka-6 sailplane that proved to be a good performance match with my new friend Wally Scott's Schweizer 1-26. We began a series of friendly competitions, and, on days when we did not fly cross country, we flew locally, having last man down or shortest landing distance contests. I was impressed when I learned that Wally carried a recording barograph, on even our local flights, and that he analyzed the trace to determine how he could have improved his performance that day. Here was a man who was serious about improving his flying skills and, hence, his flights.

As our soaring skills improved, our friendship grew and, as the summers passed, I became the east-coast member of the Scott family, with visits in the evenings to Wally at the Scott Theater often preceded by a delightful meal prepared by Wally's wife Boots. Sailplane performance was improving dramatically with the advent of fiberglass construction, and Wally and I moved up periodically as newer models became available. The summer of 1970 arrived with both of us flying Schleicher ASW-12s, a German design with excellent performance for its time. Our world record flight that summer to Columbus, Nebraska was probably the highlight of my soaring career, but Wally, who tells the story of our flight in this book, went on to accomplish many outstanding distance flights in the years that followed. I remember him as a great friend, a fine soaring companion, and a superb pilot who confronted the challenges of flying sailplanes long distances and conquered them with skill and grace.

Ben Greene, White Lake, NC 2010

Preface

It was passion, dedication of the highest form, and perhaps a calling of sorts that kept Wallace A. Scott flying for thirty-five years, covering over 303,000 miles of cross-country gliding. This was a man who woke up every summer morning, climbed onto the roof of his house and looked southward to the cumulus clouds to decide whether it would be a good flying day. Committing himself to gliding at every sunrise, Wally did not miss any opportunity to fly.

One of the soaring community's foremost glider pilots, Wally, and a select few, changed the face of gliding and what it meant to be a glider pilot. A mere sixty years since Otto Lilienthal and the Wright brothers' first experimentation with engineless and motorized flight, Wally was among the first wave of soaring legends. Of Wally, fellow glider pilot Jim Callaway says, 'He was truly at the focal point of international gliding, and he was astute enough to recognize the benefits of making it all work in Odessa, Texas.'

Winning the Barringer Trophy, soaring's preeminent award for distance, twenty times in a twenty-six-year span, Wally made the relatively unknown Barringer the ultimate free-distance achievement. On an international level, Wally set four world gliding records, participated in two World Championships and was the only man in the world to have held all recognized world distance records simultaneously. As gliding friend Sherman Griffith remembers, 'The most impressive part is that Wally started setting these world records after only a few years as a glider pilot.'

Ultimately his accomplishments in the sport would gain Wally induction to the Helms Soaring Hall of Fame in 1965, which later became the US Soaring Hall of Fame, and Wally's 1-35A sailplane would be on display at the Smithsonian Institute of Air and Space Museum in Washington D.C.

More important to Wally than the world records and stream of awards was the chance to live a life dedicated to the pursuit of soaring 1,000 miles of free distance, which to this day has not been done by an American glider pilot. Wally would come close with a final out-and-return flight of 808 miles in 1998, but ultimately age and a lifetime of soaring would catch up to him and the dream of 1,000 miles would live on in those he inspired. The amount of work and commitment to soaring Wally displayed in his lifetime is best summed up by fellow glider pilot Marion Griffith, 'It's hardship to fly 6- or 700 miles in a glider, it's tough to do it, really hard work and if you haven't had to show true grit you'll never be able to do it and Wally Scott wasn't scared to show what he was made of.'

I came to write about Wally Scott through one who calls Wally his mentor, Mark Huffstutler. On a visit to Texas, Mark offered me, what was then referred to as a 'summer project' but would prove to be slightly more involved. As a student living in Boston, I leapt at the chance to escape the city and get back to the West. I never had a chance to meet Wally, but I came to know him through his own writings, his magazine articles and his extensive journals where he also writes about his World War II experiences.

In visits to Odessa, I spent time with the other half of Wally's team, his wife, Boots. Boots revealed to me the ingredients of a good life according to the Scotts; the largest part being the choice of the right life mate. Wally's life centered on flying, family and his desire to devote his life so fully to both resulted in a daily balancing act. Sometimes a struggle, Wally never let one overwhelm the other. Each potentially flyable day began with a trip up to the roof, a look to the south and, if he saw Cu's, a call down to Boots. It was a good day to fly.

PART 1 – THE FIRST LEG: 1924 - 1946

Forever Plus Two Days

Gray clouds threatened from the northwest horizon toward Odessa, Texas. As we got closer, the storm encircled the Barron until the decision to turn back came from the seat next to me. 'Call Boots.' Mark said. 'Tell her we're socked in, and we'll have to try again later in the week.' To be honest, I was relieved. I was nervous to meet part of the story I would be writing about and didn't know quite what to expect. I picked up my cell phone from the center console and wondered what to say to the 78-year-old woman who was probably already waiting at the airport. Then I realized anything I said to Boots about flying would be understood. A seasoned pilot's wife, Boots knew far better than I, that when it comes to flying, everything is dependant on the weather.

Our second flight, a few days later, brought us safely into Schlemeyer/Odessa Airport where Boots Scott was waiting on the ground. I barely got out of the plane before I was wrapped in Boots' great arms and greeted with a Southern drawl and her, 'Hello Sweetie.' Boots said a quick hello to Mark, turned to face me and said, 'Well, come on!' I opened the door to her Mercury Monterey, waved goodbye to Mark and slid in beside Boots. Rightly so, the tour began with the airport where Wally had spent half of his life. We drove by two, now empty hangars where he had kept his gliders and Boots began to talk of Wally's first love, flying. The drive through Odessa took us past the site of the old Plains drive-in theater that Wally ran for 20 years. A red-brick bank building now stands in its place. Further southeast on our drive, we passed the former Scott and Rio Theater sites, the Scott family's downtown theaters. Low-level apartments now reside where the Rio once stood, and the Scott theater sits empty and decaying. Boots looped around town to Permian High School where Wally and Boots' children attended high school. Between landmarks, I saw flat countryside and highways that go on forever in every direction, just like any other post-boom town in west Texas.

As we pulled up to the Scott family home, I could see a glider trailer down the right side of the driveway. The left side of the driveway was taken over by an RV, the calling card of the gilder pilot. Due to the large size of the RV, only the front half of the house was visible from this direction. We pulled in behind the glider accessories to an almost-hidden back door. Archery bows and arrows lined the outside of the house around the driveway. 'Did Wally used to shoot?' I asked Boots. 'Oh yes, we both did.' she said. 'We won the husband and wife Texas team trophy, but I'll tell you about that later,' Boots casually waived off the statement with her arm. 'Come on inside now,' she said.

According to Boots, the house feels much the same way it did when the kids were in high school. Family pictures grace the walls of the living room and completely cover the top of the baby grand piano. The couches in the living room are placed in an L shape against the wall and close to the dining room to leave space in the center of the house. An extra refrigerator stocked with sodas sits right inside the back door of the garage. If you take a closer look, all you see is Wally. Model sailplanes hang from the ceiling in the TV room, and more than half of the pictures in the house have a glider in the background. On every desk, in every drawer, in a piece of furniture meant for dishes, are stacks of Wally's writing, Wally's awards, and Wally's legacy.

Boots showed me to Wally Jr's old room where I would sleep for the night. I placed my bag down by the bookshelf and quickly scanned the titles on the lowest shelf. American history books, issues of Soaring Magazine and flying books by Dr. Ernest Steinhoff and Joseph Lincoln featuring Wally lay slightly cluttered on the shelf. "Come on back to the living room, and we'll talk," Boots called from down the hall. I grabbed my tape recorder, paper and a pen and joined her in the living room.

Boots invited me to sit next to her on the white and gold sofa. She smiled at the prospect of telling me her story. She sat with her legs crossed and angled her upper body toward me. Her hands sat folded together in her lap. 'What do you want to know about first?' Boots began the interview with a question to me.

I shifted somewhat uncomfortably on the couch and tried to get one leg under me so I could face her. 'Tell me what you loved most about Wally, and then we'll start at the beginning.'

Her eyes became a little teary, 'I loved so much about this man,' she said. 'I'll love him forever plus two days, just as he always said to me. Here's just a little of my Wallace.'

Over the next four hours, I hardly had to ask a question or redirect the conversation. Boots introduced me to Wally's own writings about his childhood and described her world of family and flying. The words tow plane, cu, free distance and Barringer fall second nature from her mouth… an acquired language and lifestyle picked up over many years of following and growing with Wallace and the intrigue of soaring.

First Came Dixie

On Independence Day, July 4, 1924, just as a train rumbled through Van Horn, Texas, Wallace Aiken Scott came into the world. 'No wonder I have always liked choo-choo trains,' he writes. 'When I became a man, my priorities of ownership were an airplane, a car, and an electric train.' The first item on this list would prove to be a lifelong passion, while trains would remain a fragment of childhood.

Wally joined two brothers and two sisters in the enterprising Scott family whose business, while homesteading in the Sierra Diablo Mountains, consisted of enterprises in art, the confectionary business and even a try at a grocery and drug store. Wally's father, Claude Winfred Scott, was known to be a talented painter and art dealer. Maggie Elizabeth Scott, who spent over thirty years raising children, would later become the president of Scott Industries when the family entered the movie theater business.

The written history of Van Horn, Texas makes mention of the C.W. Scott family as pioneers of this area. They left Van Horn in 1926 when Wally was two years old and headed to Best, Texas, looking for the next possibly successful venture. While in Best, the family operated the only motion picture theater and began working in an industry that would remain with the Scotts throughout Wally's entire life. The Scotts spent only a few short months in Best, Texas, an oil boom town that no longer exists. A road sign in the area is the only proof that it was once there. As the gushing oil wells began to dry up, they were forced to move to Iraan, Texas.

Iraan, a contraction of the names of the local oil magnate Ira Yates and his wife Ann, would prove to be a boom town right up to the gloom of the depression. The Scotts spent ten years in Iraan, the formative years of Wally's life.

Wally described Iraan as, 'the perfect representative for a swash-buckling, bigger than life boom town.' The streets were crowded at all hours of the day, and the theater that Wally's father built, the Dixie, was paid for in short order at ten cents a ticket. In a few years, the Dixie would be turned into a recreation hall after Claude Scott built a more modern theater across the street. In a few more years, this theater too would be replaced with a newer and larger theater a few doors west of the old Dixie.

The newest theater housed 600 to 700 people, had a larger balcony, and a completely fireproof projection room that Wally's oldest brother, Lawrence, designed. Lawrence, nicknamed Bud, was the projectionist at all the theaters. After fighting several booth fires as a projectionist and being injured, Bud knew it was in his best interest to create a fireproof projection room.

The four Scott children would rise in the early morning hours to clean, mop and sweep the theater. Bud was in charge of shipping film, preparing new film and driving the car with its banner advertising the theater, while barking out the show information through a megaphone to everyone on the streets. During this time, the Scott family lived in the old tin building that used to be the Dixie. While the old metal siding would moan, creak, snap, and pop in the wind, most children found comfort sleeping with a light on. Not Wally. He believed that if a boogey man came looking for him, he wanted it totally dark to make it harder to find him.

Even during his childhood, Wally had the self-assurance and fearlessness of a soldier at war, ready for whatever battle was next to be fought. It would be some time before Wally's strengths would be tested at war, but his years as a Texan youngster in the 1930s Wild West would prepare him for some of life's toughest battles.

Hollywood Be Thy Name

Wallace Scott, Personal Journal, February 4, 1985

"No one taught me how to smoke; I learned it myself. Our theater customers who smoked couldn't do so inside because of the building structure, so they would throw their cigarettes away before entering the theater. One night, I picked up a couple of butts and retired to my favorite easy chair, which happened to be the running board of a Model A Ford.

"I knew nothing about inhaling, so I sat there in my reclined position puffing away. After blowing out two or three times, a guy flipped a half-used Roi Tan cigar in my direction. I was taken with the artistry and color of the band. It did taste and smell a little bit different, and I thought I was the cat's meow with that big stogie. That is until I started getting sick and the world started going round in circles. I suddenly wanted my mother, but couldn't seem to navigate very well or even stand up for that matter.

"Meanwhile, a small search party had been initiated and people were being recruited to help find me. In a time before street lights in our neighborhood, I managed to be invisible at no more than thirty feet away. Once I was discovered and cured by my mother and a couple bouts of getting sick, I swore off tobacco until I was eighteen. By that time everybody was doing it too, and I forced myself—only to be part of the crowd.

"After a small scolding for my smoking incident, I returned to the inside of our theater where a full audience sat watching *Wings*. I can still feel the excitement those early flying films built up in me. It was the speed, effortlessness and amazement of flying through the eyes of Hollywood. Hollywood was everything then, even a part of my prayers.

"When my older brother, Oliver Elwood, and I shared a double bed, he spent many nights saying his prayers out loud, so that I could learn them. Gee, to me Hollywood must be important, I thought…if we referred to it in our Lord's Prayer. Oliver knelt by the side of the bed with his palms pressed together and said, 'Our Father, who art in Heaven, *Hollywood* be thy name. Thy kingdom come. Thy will be done, on Earth as it is in Heaven.' I never found out until years later that Hollywood didn't have quite the holy quality the word *hallowed* there is meant to imply.

"In September of 1930, I started spending the bulk of my time at the Iraan Pecos County Independent School Districts' class room for first graders. I remember how my feet felt after not having worn shoes for practically my whole life. My feet felt like they were burning off. Every spring and every September it was the same. In September, there was 'new shoes day' or 'good used shoes day' and in late May and through the summer it became 'barefoot day.' It was the same every year, and each May it became just a little tougher to get used to the very rocky soils, gobs of puncture veins, and grass burrs that defined Iraan. My Mother always said, "When the going gets tough, gritting your teeth might help." Her advice carried me through many a barefoot summer in Iraan.

22 Short

A childhood prone to the outdoors, Wally spent his youth climbing mountains, exploring nearby caves and looking for trouble in town. By the age of seven or eight, some young Texas boys like Wally had 22-short single shot rifles. They would hike up to their favorite caves and shoot down at the river below, making the water splash into miniature geysers. The boys would attempt to shoot at birds, but never really succeeded because of their amateur shots and inefficient rifles.

One day however, Wally shot a jack rabbit in a cave. Being the adventuresome lot that they were, the boys decided they were going to put the jackrabbit onto a spit and barbecue it over an open flame, just like cowboys in a western did. They managed to get the jackrabbit on a stick by shoving it right down the rabbit's throat. After some disagreement as to whether or not to skin the rabbit, they ultimately decided the fire would burn the skin off anyway, so they decided to leave it on. The fur caught fire and started turning everything black. One of the more aggressive of the foursome grabbed a handful of dirt and tossed it onto the flaming rabbit.

Once the fire was out, they continued to rotate the carcass, their mouths watering with anticipation at what they expected would be a delectable meal. After several minutes, stuff started oozing out of the rabbits mouth and other orifices and the boy's appetites began to wane. Another ten minutes went by before Wally decided the rabbit must be ready to eat. They picked the blackened rabbit out of the fire and began to argue over who would take the first bite. Showing a natural affinity for pragmatism, Wally decided they would all take a bite at the same time. The boys sat in a circle, two on each side of the rabbit and said, 'On the count of three. Three, two, one – bite!' The foul taste of the burned rabbit carcass can only be qualified by the fact that Wally never ate rabbit again.

Unfortunately burnt rabbit comes at a near second to the worst item Wally ate during his years in Iraan and most likely ever in his life. The Scott family dining table was a large round American style table with claw feet at the base of the center pedestal. Wally found the table to be an incredibly prosperous site for chewing gum. All members of the Scott family chewed gum, which meant that the underside of the table was constantly covered. When no one was looking, Wally would peel the week-old gum off the table and plop it in his mouth. There were times, however, when Wally needed gum and the gum from the dining room table couldn't be procured. He found a substitute. On the walk home from school one afternoon Wally and his friend were walking by a construction site where the plumbing was being worked on. The plumber had taken a chisel to tear away large chunks of lead to melt for sealing purposes. Wally asked the plumber for a chunk of the lead. The lead went directly from his hand into his mouth.

The taste of lead was not exactly like regular gum, but it was acceptable. The lead could be chewed, and it produced a gum-like amount of juices. Wally spit the juices out occasionally, but most of the time he went right ahead and swallowed them. To his knowledge, Wally never felt the effects of the poisonous lead.

In the age of the Roaring '20s and '30s, flappers and Prohibition, rumble-seat automobiles and Einstein's brand new theory of relativity, Wally was wandering the streets of Iraan chewing lead. Besides school, his friends and the rest of the Scott family, Wally's reality existed through the myriad of flying movies he frequented. Flying was just starting to become popular as both a hobby and a profession. Since the invention of the 'flying machine' just 25 years ago, airplanes had come a long way since the Wright brothers, but the actual idea of being able to fly was a somewhat distant desire.

For now, the simple feeling of being weightless and moving at relatively high speeds would have to suffice. As Wally experimented with sliding, jumping and diving wherever he could, he would discover there were benefits to believing in divine protection when performing dangerous feats. Valuing faith would remain a huge part of Wally's life and especially during his flying where long hours in flights across the country and the world would place him in trying situations.

Foundations of Faith

Wallace Scott, Personal Journal, February 20, 1995

"A new drug store across the street from the old Dixie Theater had installed new glass topped display cases and counter tops. The old counters had been discarded into the vacant lot next door where I was climbing around on them and sliding down the tops. I would run and gather speed and then land and slide across the old countertops. It was about the nearest thing to ice skating I had ever discovered.

"I had no idea how dangerous this was. I was one hard fall away from getting severely injured. All of a sudden, I saw a boy standing there watching me. He was a nice looking boy and about a head taller than me. He wanted to know what I was doing and asked if I knew how dangerous it was. I brushed the idea away and asked him to come join me. He said he'd rather not and he continued to stand there and talk to me.

'Where ya from?' I asked after a minute or so.

'I'm not from around here, my parents are in visiting friends,' he said. 'What do you like to do?'

'Well, I like to play cowboys and Indians. Tom Mix and Hoot Gibson are my favorites.'

'Yeah, I like them too,' the boy said. 'Do you believe in God?'

"I stopped my counter-top slides. No one had ever asked me this question before. Maybe my Mom and I had talked about such things and the fact that He was real and all of His teachings were real. 'Sure I believe in God!' I answered. 'Doesn't everybody?'

'No,' he said, 'No, I don't believe everybody does, but a lot of people do. But what I mean is *really* believe in God, like there couldn't even be a smidgeon of doubt. Did you know that if you really believe, and have ultimate trust, anything is possible? You could fall off this counter and land on your head and it wouldn't hurt, if you thought of your trust in Him and his protection in the instant before danger. Why don't you try it?'

"Half-heartedly I said I was game to try. 'Do you really want me to land on my head?'

"That wouldn't be necessary, he decided. We would develop my trust by lesser degrees. He told me to continue running down the top of the counter – then to fall on my rear and slide off the far end. 'But remember, you really have to believe. Remember this, in the instant before you hit the ground you have to confirm your belief and trust by concentrating on nothing else. All other thoughts will only distract you. Are you ready to try?'

"Not one to forfeit a challenge, I concentrated all I could, and ran as hard as possible and sat down on the plate glass to scoot off the far end. My legs came down on reflex and I hit the ground running.

'Do it again and this time don't put your feet down,' the boy mandated.

I repeated the run and slide. My legs didn't quite come down all the way, and I hit pretty hard.

'Did that hurt?' he asked.

'Not really,' I said kind of surprised it hadn't hurt, but not really too sure what the boy was trying to accomplish.

'This time I want you to run as fast as you can and slide off the table with your legs pointed straight ahead. Don't bring them down and take the full brunt of the force on your seat. But, in the instance before you hit think of your trust in Him. Will you do that for me?'

28

"Yes I would, and I was excited by his guarantee that I would not get hurt. Nothing quite like this had ever happened to me before, and I couldn't understand all of what was happening. I went to the end of the counter and blasted off as fast as I could, literally leaping into the air from my sliding position. My legs remained fully extended and, in the instant before colliding with Mother Earth, I asked for divine protection, and I got it. I hadn't felt a thing. Nothing.

"This was incredibly frightening, as I could not explain what had just happened. I conjecture that this was the beginning of my faith—a faith that has gotten me through the challenges of my life. Most importantly, however, it was my faith that kept me company on all those distance flights in the glider, and it was my faith that kept allowing me to get back in the glider after my trust could have been destroyed."

Bud, Barnstormers and Ballyhooing

The Scott children were an active, boisterous bunch, but the family theater kept them all grounded. Wally's older brother, Oliver Elwood, took his place as the local Friday-night, high-school football hero. The year before the Scott family would move to Odessa, Texas, Oliver scored five touchdowns to help Iraan beat Odessa 48-0. When he wasn't playing football, Oliver and Wally's oldest sister, Winnie, ran the ticket booth at the theater and sold popcorn when it got busy. Agnes, the middle child of the five, was in charge of the old player piano down by the screen. In the days of silent films, the choices were either the player piano or hiring a pianist to accompany the film, which was considerably more expensive. Right up until around 1933, when the film industry began replacing the player piano with 78 rpm records, Wally would spend time everyday helping Agnes.

The Scott parents had their hands full running the theater and watching their children get into minor trouble in Iraan. But during the summer of 1934, Claude and Maggie would face a bigger challenge. Claude was diagnosed with a ruptured groin and heart problems. Bud would have to take over most aspects of the theater, working sunup to sundown in order to keep the family afloat. Bud had already been entrusted with the most responsibility, but at this point he became the man of the family. 'He bore these obligations with an air of charm and dedication toward us all,' Wally writes.

In the meantime, Bud had met a young girl named Dorothy Watson, whom he later married. They had a daughter named Lodema M. Scott. Bud had three loves besides Dorothy and Lodema: airplanes, cars, and guns. Whenever a stunt pilot, then called a 'barnstormer', would come to town to show off their stuff, Bud would spend his daily salary for a five-minute ride. He devoured everything he could read on the subject and even ordered a kit plane to build in his spare time. Bud wanted to fly so badly that Oliver and Wally had no choice but to be intrigued right along with him.

On one afternoon in June, an old Ford Tri-Motor plane came buzzing around town at low altitude advertising that he could hop passengers from the airport in McCamey to Iraan. Bud grabbed Wally, borrowed five dollars from their mother, and away they went to McCamey for Wally's very first airplane ride.

The flight in the old Tri-Motor, one of only 199 to be produced, would prove to be a life changing experience for 10-year-old Wallace Scott. Once on board the airplane nicknamed 'The Tin Goose,' Wally found a single row of seats on either side of the cabin, and a walkway down the center. The seats were old, wicker-woven chairs that had been bolted to the floor and had minimal back and bottom cushions. From the row of windows alongside the chairs, Wally watched as the world below seemed to creep by, even at 100 miles an hour. The flight lasted for an unforgettable ten minutes. 'Yes,' Wally decided, 'I must own one of these someday.' He thought about how airplanes would replace cars, and soon the advertising of the time would hail, 'An airplane for every garage.' This dream of Wally's, however, would have to wait for a better economy.

In 1934, as President Roosevelt enacted a complex series of economic programs known as the New Deal to bring the country out of a worsening economic state, the effects of the Depression were making a visible mark on the town of Iraan. Show business had dropped off so dramatically that the Scott family started Bank Night, where they had to give money away in order to make any. Each week a drawing was held for a $25 giveaway, but you had to be present to win. If the winner was not present, another $25 would be added to the pot to make the prize $50 the next week, and so on.

When the pot grew to $100 or more, it was considered to be big money. In the summer of 1934, the pot got to be $300, and people came from near and far until there was standing room only in the theater. It nearly bankrupted the theater, however, as 700 or 800 admissions at fifteen cents a ticket only adds up to $120, and here they were giving away $300.

Show business was bad, but prosperity was right around the corner. FDR's New Deal programs were beginning to have a positive effect on the economic climate, and the hardest part was over, but nobody knew that yet. In order to make ends meet, the Scotts built a new drugstore alongside the Dixie Theater. The two buildings were situated such that one could go directly from the theater into the drugstore. An innovative idea, the Scotts were a little ahead of their time, and the drugstore failed before the Depression was over. Seventy-five percent of what once was Iraan had been lost. The Scott family was forced to sell the theaters and all other properties they owned. Bud, Dorothy and Lodema packed up and moved to Ozona, Texas to try their luck there. They opened a very small theater called the Paramount, which Bud ran mostly on his own. The Paramount soon failed, and Bud, now 28, was forced to move his family back to Iraan.

The quality of life in Iraan was not improving, and Claude's health was failing quickly. In May of 1936, the family convinced him to go to a hospital in San Angelo, Texas, where he would have an operation. While in the hospital, Claude got a staph infection and required a major blood transfusion. Bud and Oliver rushed up to San Angelo to donate blood to their father. After the transfusions, their father perked up immediately.

Once Claude seemed to be steadily improving, the boys headed back to Iraan. Three days later, Bud had to go back to the hospital. During the direct blood transfusion, some of Claude's blood was accidentally pumped directly into Bud, and the effect was devastating. In less than a week, Bud was dead. The Scott family suffered not only the loss of their eldest son and brother, but also the main source of income for the entire family. Claude remained on his sickbed, as his family fell to pieces around him.

To twelve-year-old Wally, the loss of his oldest brother and largest childhood influence was nothing short of devastating. On the day of Bud's death, Wally had been told that Bud had 'passed on,' which caused some confusion. Wally understood the dynamics of life and had encountered death before, but he had no idea what a friend of his mother's had meant in saying 'passed on.' It took Wally the length of the car ride to figure out what the words most likely meant. Once realized, he immediately began to pray that he was wrong.

In Wally's own words, the Scott family recovery was nothing short of remarkable. They had hit bottom, and now there was only one direction to go. So, as Wally wrote, 'we rolled up our sleeves and started climbing.' The first big decision, instituted by the newly appointed matriarchal board of directors, was to leave Iraan. Wally's mother, Maggie, and his sisters, Winnie and Agnes, concluded that Iraan did not offer the opportunities that were called for at this time. Just like Best and so many other oil towns, Iraan had 'boomed' and was in the process of going 'bust.' Maggie Scott arranged to dispose of all properties that were left, closed up shop, and purchased a '35 Ford. Maggie, Winnie and Agnes drove around Texas looking for the next place to move. In a close decision, Odessa beat out countless other potential towns. With a net worth of $300, the Scott family loaded up the Ford and headed to Odessa.

Odessa had a brand new theater, The Aztec, which had been built in the last year or two and then closed down due to the competition of the Hodge family. The Hodge family owned many theaters in the area and were considered formidable competition. Maggie arranged a meeting with Mr. Henderson, the owner of The Aztec, and discussed her desire to re-open the theater. Mr. Henderson took a liking to the spunkiness of the Scott women. He struck a deal with them that would ultimately save the Scotts. He charged them $8,000 for a new and fully equipped modern theater made of brick and mortar. With no down payment required, Mr. Henderson left with, "Just pay me when you can."

The next months were spent renovating The Aztec. Bud's young family, Dorothy and Lodema, had moved to Kansas and in with Dorothy's mother, and it would be some time before they returned. Claude would stay in the hospital in San Angelo for a few more months. The remaining Scotts renamed The Aztec, The Rio Theater. On opening night, the blazing new neon lights lit up the new theater. It was an overnight success. The whole town of Odessa was booming. Stores stayed open in the downtown area all night long as the birth of 24-hour grocery stores and cafés took flight.

Wally was in charge of popcorn at the theater. Like any 12-year-old, he hated working on the weekends when his friends were out playing. In late summer of 1936, Claude returned from San Angelo to a flourishing business. He continued to be as productive as he could, but he was never the same. The Rio Theater was well underway, and the film business in general was thriving. Sound and color improvements made Hollywood blockbusters the highlight of the entertainment industry. *Gone With the Wind* (1939) was just around the corner, and stars like Shirley Temple, Will Rogers and Fred Astaire were lighting up the silver screen. The Rio Theater was paid off in less than a year. Finally, the Scotts were achieving success in the industry to which they had devoted thirty years of their lives.

Oliver, now nicknamed Scotty, went off to Texas Tech on a partial football scholarship; he then went on to the University of Texas at Arlington. Once he had finished his education, he came home to Odessa and joined the CPT (Civilian Pilot Training) program. He spent a couple of months at the airfield in Big Spring, Texas, and became an instructor for the class of 1942 at Ft. Stockton, Texas. Wally would follow in his brother's path a few years later.

In 1941, the Scotts built a new theater to rival a theater modestly named 'The Texas' that their chief competitors, the Hodges, had built. The Scott's new theater was slightly larger and a bit nicer. Throughout high school, Wally worked part-time at the theater and got into trouble when he could. One night while being chased by friends in a drag race referred to as 'ditch'em,' Wally turned off the lights on the theater pick-up truck to try to outrun and loose his buddies. In the midst of the darkened chase, Wally hit a guy wire for the power lines and knocked out all of the electricity in West Odessa. A sheriff caught him and, much to his humiliation, they called his mother and Scotty who had to come and bail him out of jail where he had been kept in a holding cell. Wally continued to spend most of his time driving the theater pick-up around, but he never drove with the lights off again. Wally loved that theater pick-up and was certain that if it had been outfitted with wings it would have flown.

As high school wore on and America was knee-deep in World War II, Wally took an interest in the war effort. He began to question some of his activities and his everyday lifestyle in Odessa. Although he loved Odessa, Wally decided he needed a change of scenery. He attended Schreiner Military Academy in Kerrville, Texas. Schreiner proved to be an ideal setting for Wally's need of change. A break from the games of ditch'em and getting into trouble at home, Wally found himself taking long walks along the riverbanks and learning how to water ski and other water sports he would continue to love for the rest of his life.

It wasn't just the long walks by the river, the sports, or his studies that provided Wally with the means to forge a deeper understanding of himself and his place in the world. It was on his daily walks around and across campus that he learned how to bring God into his moments of self-reflection. He found this difficult at first, but with some practice and a little focus it developed into a habit. Wally found himself making promises that he would try to keep until his last days.

Toward the end of the summer, Wally found out that his mother had bought a Piper J-2 Cub for Scotty and himself. The American-built J-2 Cub was a two-seat, light aircraft and the first of many successful Piper Cub designs. Wally learned to fly at Fort Stockton, TX where Scotty could teach him. This opportunity to learn to fly would provide the perfect culmination to the past year at Schreiner. In the fall, Wally decided to start taking classes at the high school in Fort Stockton, mainly in aviation.

Second Nature

Wallace Scott, Personal Journal, February 28, 1995

"When I left Odessa, the remains of my past life stayed in the past. A new course for my being had been chartered, not by me, but by fate. The thought didn't come to me at first, but Scotty and I were to do the exact things that Bud had always dreamt of doing. There was little doubt about him being with us; if not in reality, certainly in memory.

"Scotty took me to Win-Field airport, which at the time was the civilian field at Fort Stockton. The military field, Gibbs Field, was off-limits to civilians and private aircraft. Here at Win-Field, I met Wes Stoddard for the first time. Wes was an instructor for the army and managed Win-Field on the side.

"As Mother and Scotty had purchased the J-2 Cub from Wes, it was only right to allow him to introduce me to the machine. It was beautiful. Painted Cub yellow, the ship was ten years old and the engine had over four thousand hours logged, but it looked brand new. Wes, an accomplished aircraft mechanic, had kept the Continental 4-banger with 37 horsepower in perfect condition. Turning 2,800 rpm at cruise, it sounded like a fine tuned watch. The total cost for our first J-2 was $400. Today, in the same shape, the cub would be worth more than $30,000.

"Stoddard took Scotty and me around the machine and introduced us to all the control features and the lack of some. It had no airspeed indicator, and we would have to use the tachometer for an indicator. It had no wheel brakes, but did have a directional control steerable tail wheel. We would have to keep taxiing speeds slow. The throttle was a long guided bar running from the back seat to the front. There were no navigation lights or landing lights, so night flying would be forbidden.

"The good news was the speed of flight. Climb, cruise, or glide, the J-2 would fly at about 50 mph. If you used the highways for navigation purposes, you'd better be prepared to be outrun by all the traffic going your direction. Even the old trucks would rush past you from below. Everything considered, however, it was a beautiful machine, and you couldn't beat the chance to be in the air.

"Scotty and I prepared to take it up for our first flight. Scotty explained how we would inspect the plane very meticulously every time we would fly. We began at the left side by the engine cowling and checked every item inside. We checked oil levels, and I learned how to properly replace the dipstick. We circled the plane and checked engine bolts, spark plugs, struts to wheels, aileron attachments, vertical fins, rudder movement, and ten minutes later we ended where we started and checked the propeller for damage.

"I climbed into the front seat and Scotty made his way into the rear. Wes went to the front of the Cub to give us a hand in propping {sic} to start the engine. There was no electrical way to start the Cub. It had to be started by hand. From the back seat, I heard a voice yell, 'relax, just follow through, listen and learn.' Wes and Scotty called back and forth to one another in a succession of pilot commands 'gas on, switch off, throttle closed, brakes set, throttle full closed no brakes,' and finally Scotty called back, 'switch on, no brakes, retarded throttle, contact.' Wes then pulled the propeller through with impulse, and the little Continental purred to life.

"Scotty told me to watch his taxiing techniques and throttle coordination for taxi speed control. 'We never want to taxi too fast, even if we had brakes,' he said, 'Remember this, a great deal of learning to fly will be by repetition. We will do everything over and over again, until it becomes like second nature.'

"Scotty made a slow 360-degree clearing turn to make sure we were free of incoming traffic. He gradually aligned the nose of the J-2 into the wind and advanced the throttle to maximum rpm. He called the tachometer to my attention and the little needle was resting on 3,000 revolutions per minute. We started down the runway and slowly began to climb off the ground.

'At full throttle and at proper climb speed, we will show 3,000 rpm on the tachometer. If we pull the nose up slightly the airspeed will slow down, and this will affect the revolutions of the prop. It will decrease,' Scotty instructed. He demonstrated and, sure enough, when he pulled the nose of the little ship into a barely perceptible steeper climb mode, you could hear the air noise and see the revs diminishing on the tachometer. To me, this was about as clear as mud.

"Scotty reassured me, 'Don't worry now about all this. We are on your introductory ride, so just relax and enjoy it. A lot of this will straighten out with ground school.' I started to relax a bit. 'Isn't this fun little brother? I just know you are going to love it! I'll make a deal with you. I will teach you the best way I know how to fly, if you promise me that you will learn the best way you know how. Working together, we should be able to make you one hell of a good pilot. Do we have a deal?'

'We've got a deal,' I shouted back.

'Why don't you take the controls—don't grip them, just relax. We won't fall out of the air. Follow me through on the controls, and I will demonstrate control movements. Notice how our wings are level on the horizon; each wing tip is exactly the same distance above the horizon as the other. Look and check for yourself, you can relax and look around. We still won't fall out of the air; the airplane will do what you want it to do. As pilot, you are the master. Always remember that. Be kind and gentle and accurate, and the little ship will respond to your every desire.'

"I thought to myself about how beautiful this was. No wonder people like flying. 'You know Scotty, I was just thinking to myself how much Bud would have liked doing what we're doing.'

'I know,' Scotty said.

"Scotty asked me to try some gentle turns and told me that we wanted to do all maneuvers as accurately as possible. He led me through some 90-degree turns and taught me how to roll right and left immediately with a 45-degree bank to another 45-degree bank. After a little over an hour of flying, Scotty told me to head back to Win-Field. He let me take a few gliding turns before he took over and brought us in for landing. I received a fair report once we had laid the J-2 to rest and immediately headed to the chalkboard where more questions would be asked and explained. On October 2, 1942, the day after my introductory flight O.E., Scotty logged for W.A. Scott thirty minutes of dual in Cub J-2."

Whiskey Alpha

With Scotty as his instructor, Wally quickly took to flying. During the year of 1942, Wally spent his days taking classes at Fort Stockton, followed by five or six hours of flying. He returned to Odessa regularly with Scotty where they were able to fly in peace without the cadets crowding Win-Field. World War II was beginning to heat up and, on January 26th, the first American forces arrived in Europe. America was now locked into the greatest war in history. In a move that would allow the town to profit immensely, the lazy airfield in Midland, Texas, became the Midland Army Air Field, one of the largest training bases in the world at the time. The Army Air Forces Bombardier-training school began operation at Midland in 1942 with over 10,000 permanent employees and soldiers. Another large bomber training field was located in Pyote, Texas. Every hour, buses were arriving in Odessa from both fields. This was full-fledged war, and all Wally had to do was look around to know it.

Wally's friends, who were still left in Odessa and who had not gone to war, would often fly with Wally, even before he had a license. While illegal, Wally would write it off saying, 'we wouldn't have done it except for the fun. If a guy couldn't have a little fun now and then, perhaps the times would appear too grim to bear.' Beating the war sodden attitude of the time, Wally and his friends would go to Ector County Airport and Wally would take-off. His friends would wait a few minutes and then drive off to meet him in a secret location on some nearby ranch road or oil field where he would land and take them for a flight, one at a time. The boys would climb into the plane, each with a sack of flour in hand pinched from their mother's pantries. Wally would fly relatively close to the ground, and the boys would scour the countryside looking for jackrabbits, coyotes, or any hapless cows below. Once the target was spotted, the plane would erupt in 'let's get'em cries.' When the J-2 was at the right distance and angle from the animal, one boy would unlatch the window, stick his arm out with a sack of flour in hand, count to three and drop. The little sack of flour would drop from the plane, and, on a lucky shot, it would burst all over the animal target. Overseas, A-12 bombs dropped on Germany. Over Odessa, Texas flour sacks made their mark on the countryside.

On a more peaceful flight in the J-2, Wally took off from Ector County just as the first rays of the sun warmed the eastern horizon. The air was still; there was not a ripple of motion in the space surrounding the yellow Cub. Set free, the J-2 climbed higher and higher into the grays and blues of the dawn. Up here, Wally found nothing but sublime peace. The J-2 seemed to thrive on the rarefied atmosphere, climbing higher than the frame of the small airplane should've allowed.

Wally took control back from the J-2 and cut the power slowly, gradually bringing the throttle back to reduce the rpm's so the engine wouldn't cool too quickly and suffer internal stress. Wally finally reached the point where he could close the throttle no further. He reached up and turned the magneto switch to the off position and slowed the airspeed to a near stall. The propeller came to a standstill. Now they were a glider. It would take the rest of the morning to lose all the altitude they had gained.

Wally had his hands inside his jacket, slightly nudging his knee against the control stick. The J-2 responded obediently to the guidance. Outside, the air temperature was well below zero. Turning off the engine also meant the end of cabin heat. They would continue losing altitude, and soon their glide would be over. Wally increased airflow over the propeller by lowering the nose slightly, and the prop began to move with the increasing airspeed. With a shudder, the yellow Cub came to life again, and the running engine brought heat back into the Cub's cabin.

After putting the J-2 in the hangar, Wally reached into the Cub's side pocket for his logbook. He logged the flight and commented on the perfection of the sunrise mission. As he left the hangar, Wally turned to glance back at the J-2 and thought he could detect a slight smile emanating from the face-like features of the little airplane.

In January of 1943, Wally and Scotty sold the great little J-2 back to Wes Stoddard for exactly what they had paid for it. They had put some wear and tear on the aircraft, but it was still in very good condition. Scotty bought the Fort Stockton detachment of the Scott family a new airplane with 100% help from their mother. The Culver Cadet was much faster and more comfortable, but the J-2 would remain close to being Wally's favorite for the rest of his life. The memory of engineless flight in the happy yellow Cub would stay with Wally until years later, when once again, it would be without an engine that Wally would fly at his best.

Despite a few learners' mistakes, Wally finished his training hours and obtained his pilot's license. Following in his older brother's footsteps, Wally went straight into Rex Chennault's instructor classes and began training to become a cadet instructor. While he was training, his salary was $200 per month, and it only took about a month to become an instructor. As an instructor, his salary jumped to $300 a month.

During his first month at Rex Chennault's flight school, Wally rented a room in a boarding house three miles from the airport. He bummed rides, took a one-dollar taxi ride or walked the hour it would take to get to the airport every morning. On a couple of occasions, Wally was late. At eighteen years old, he soon learned how to be responsible not only for himself, but also for a group of rowdy cadets.

The Best Job in the Whole Wide World

Wallace Scott, Personal Journal, March 14, 1995

"Ultimately, Rex Chennault called me into his office on one particular morning that I was late. He was very nice, but very staunch in his dealings with the student instructors. Rex was a relative of Claire Chennault who led the famed Flying Tigers, an American volunteer group of fighter pilots who helped defend China against Japan in World War II. Rex was almost as well known as Claire for his capabilities as an instructor and pilot. Rex had already talked with Scotty about my behavior and now turned to me. I kept thinking to myself, 'This is war time, certainly not play time. It's a man's world, and the real men were all wearing uniforms. Our job was to do and live if possible, but to die if necessary.' When I was called into his office, I feared the worst.

'Mr. Scott, have a seat. I'm not going to ask you your age, but I know you are still wet behind the ears. You are going to have to grow up in a hurry because these men you are to teach, they want to fly as badly as you or any instructor I have. They are willing to give up their lives in pursuit of their dreams or the job they want. It is the best job any of us could have. The best job in the whole wide world.'

"I tried not to slouch in my seat and kept my head perfectly still as he continued to talk at me.

'Mr. Scott, you have been late two or three times this past week, and I realize your mother probably let you sleep in as long as you like. Well, you can't do that here. You will be given no other chance. You must be here on time. If I were you, I would set my alarm clock an hour early because, even if you have to walk, you have to be here on time. In fact, I would buy an extra alarm clock and tell my landlady not to let me oversleep. I hope you realize how important this situation is. I would like to be a good guy and mother you a little, but the Air Corps is not built on such standards. WE ARE MEN and damned proud of it. Now get out of here, and be on time. I hope you understand everything I have said.'

"I slowly nodded my head and dazedly left his office. He was right. Welcome to the real world, I thought. I learned a lot on this day. I went to town and bought two extra alarm clocks, making three altogether. I immediately set all three of them for six a.m. I was tired. It was only 4:30 in the afternoon, but I needed a nap. I quickly told the landlady to please make sure I was up by six a.m. and that if she didn't hear me up to knock the door down. This was very important. I then took a nap, and I really needed it. I must have died, but woke up at 6:15. Hey, I'm late! The alarms didn't go off. I passed the landlady in the hall on my way out and shrugged my shoulders at her saying, 'Why did you let me oversleep?' I dashed to catch a taxi and got to base in time to clock in by 6:30, but something was wrong. Why did the clock say 18:30? I was mortified. It was the same day. The poor landlady. How would I ever apologize? I stopped by the corner drugstore on the way home and bought her a gift. It paid off after all, as she always checked on me in the morning after that.

"With the help of three alarm clocks and a little old lady knocking at my door several mornings at 6 a.m., I made my way through the instructor's classes. With Scotty's help I became an instructor at the Fort Stockton detachment of Pacific Air Schools, Ltd. A punk myself at eighteen and nineteen years old, I put through six classes of cadets in my two years as an instructor. I was a tough instructor and very demanding of my students, who were sometimes much older than I was.

"My students must have known that I was very young, as I can remember them trying to see the 1942 date on my OHS class ring. I would just twirl it around so that the ruby and date would not show. No one dared ask me my age. Not only would that have shown disrespect for me, but for the profession I represented – the best pilots in the world.

Chug-a-lugging

Wally received his sixth and last class of cadets in January of 1944. In March of the same year, he left Fort Stockton in order to advance his career as a pilot. Knowing that the primary flight school would soon be closing, many instructors had signed up to join the Ferry Command branch of the Army Air Corps. In order to join the Ferry Command, a pilot had to have a minimum of 1,000 hours logged. At this point in time, Wally had only 700 hours. He went home to Odessa for a few days before boarding a passenger train to Dallas.

When he arrived in Dallas, Wally had an appointment with the officer in charge of check rides of civilian personnel that wanted to be considered for the Ferry Command. He was 300 hours short of the 1,000 hours requirement just days before the meeting, but somehow another 300 magically appeared in his logbooks in time. The check pilot officer, however, did not ask to see his books and Wally passed his first check ride in an AT-6.

He was accepted to go to Randolph Field in San Antonio, Texas and attend flight school in order to obtain an aircraft instrument rating. Wally's training for the Ferry Command was very intensive. As things were not going well on the battlefronts in Europe and the Japanese were proving to be a fierce adversary, there was an urgency surrounding the training of new pilots for the war. Wally learned Morse code and had lots of other ground schooling that he promptly forgot.

The training graduation party was held at the Outpost Café in San Antonio. The place was full of graduates that night, and soon five giant tables had been pushed together for a chug-a-lugging contest. The game involved watching for girls going to the 'head' or powder room. It was then guessed how long she would take to re-appear. The guy farthest off would have to chug-a-lug his mug of beer. The drinking was done while the men all sang, 'Here's to Randy – he's true blue. He's a drunkard thru and thru. He's a rounder so they say. If he doesn't go to heaven, he will go the other way. So drink a chug-a-lug, chug-a-lug etc.' The training night party would not be soon forgotten, and the graduates would all head to Nashville, Tennessee in the next couple of days.

The morning after the party, as the new graduates were preparing to leave for the ferry command, Wally realized he had misplaced his shot card that contained the list of his immunizations. With two days left before the cadets were scheduled to head out, Wally had to take all his shots over again. With interns and aides coming at him from both sides with needles, Wally soon turned ash gray and was sent to his room to lie down. He never lost his shot card again.

Wally spent six weeks in Nashville under Lt. Col. Adrain P. Cote. Right at the beginning of the summer, Nashville was intensely hot and nothing was air conditioned. Wally was elected song leader of the group and then promoted to squad leader. The youngest in the group of 150, he would celebrate his twentieth birthday in Nashville one month after graduation.

After graduation, the boys all met in the barracks to select their duty stations where they would be transferred for permanent assignment. By the time Wally got to the table, most of the stations he had wanted were taken. Along with a few friends, he signed up for Palm Springs, California. There was no one lined up at the Palm Springs table and little did the boys know they had probably just chosen the greatest duty station possible.

Frank Sinatra was rumored to be based in Palm Springs, and, though Wally never met him, the whole base seemed to be swarming with famous celebrities and icons. The area was also rich in beautiful women. As the commanding officer at the time required little of his men, they spent most of the summer of 1944 checking out the women at the officer's pool. Wally's first flight away from Palm Springs was aboard a B-17 bomber. He and the captain flew the large aircraft all the way to Tucson, Arizona, where they landed, spent an hour or two on the ground, and returned to Palm Springs. There was no VIP on board, no cargo, just Wally and the captain. Both the B-17 and being based in Palm Springs were proving their worth. Wally was soon a regular co-pilot for the captains that flew out of Palm Springs. Eventually, the pilots became so comfortable with Wally, they would let him fly the entire flight, from take-off to landing.

The Scott Special

Wallace Scott, Personal Journal, April 20, 1995

"There was this American captain. He and I became about as friendly as you can get with one of these guys, unless you have a lot in common. Just the fact that you were a pilot would not let you stand out in their admiration. When the American captain and I would fly together, I would often be given the controls for landings, and I usually greased them a lot better than he did. I had youth on my side and in my favor. He must have been in his mid-fifties, which was pretty old to me at the time. Not now. Oh to be fifty-five again.

"Anyway, every time I made one of my Scott specials from the right-hand seat he became more incensed, and the worse his own landings became. On one morning flight, I noticed a wry smile come across his face, as we were on our way to 'Frisco to pick up some VIP's.

'Scott,' the captain said, 'I think I know how you have been beatin' me on all of those landings. I remember when I was a co-pilot, and I could do likewise. It all boils down to the fact that this Douglas airplane just lands better when you are sitting in the right-hand seat.'

"I could smell a rat coming—a set-up. 'Whatever you say, Cap, but that's the first time I've ever heard of that excuse.' I said and looked over at him. His hand brushed across the top of the control panel and came to point straight at me.

'Tell you what we're gonna do, Scott,' he started, 'We have no one on board so you just scrunch your little body over here, and I will play co-jockey. You're gonna be the pilot on this landing. Now don't pay too much attention that the weather is real gusty out there, and we have to come in over a sort of built-up approach at the end of the runway. It is a lot higher than the other terrain, and makes smooth landings almost impossible. Tell you what! You make one of your pebble rolling touchdowns on this landing, and I will buy you all the seafood you can eat at Fisherman's Wharf.' He glanced back to the controls for a brief second and then shot a look back at me, 'Deal?'

'What if I don't do it? What if I make one of your kind of landings?' I asked.

'Then you owe me the same meal,' he scowled.

'But I don't like seafood. I was thinking I would just have a steak finger basket. Would that be OK?'

'If that's your choice it's OK, but I know what I want. Now get over here and sit in this seat. It's put up and shut up time!' He slid off the shoulder strap to his seatbelt and started to climb out of his seat. I did the same and made it into the left-hand seat just in time to turn for final approach. The lower I got the gustier the air became, and there was a 30-degree crosswind at about 25 mph. He had me set up pretty well. Him and that big smile he'd been infected with for the past ten minutes. He was almost laughing out loud.

"'Come on Scott, you can do it,' I told myself. But the captain was right, it was pretty gusty, and I was used to flying this ship with my right hand on the yoke. I'm a lot stronger in my right arm and right now I would need all the strength I possessed. This will have to be a miracle, I thought. I called on all the strength I could assemble, but the Charlie 49 was jumping around like a West Texas bronco.

"Just as I thought I'd been beaten, everything came together at the right instant, and I could have rolled a marble for one hundred yards down the field. It was a real squealer, and perfectly smooth.

"The captain just looked at me, nearly with tears in his eyes and said, 'Damn! I wish I could do that again!'

"That night at The Wharf, the captain started to order steak fingers for me. I broke in and insisted on ordering for myself. I got a dozen oysters on the half shell and a Maine lobster as big as a small washtub. I didn't enjoy it at all, but I ate every drop and tried to smile at the same time."

The Almost P-38

During his time in Palm Springs and well after that, the Lockheed P-38 Lightning was Wally's dream plane. A precursor to the P-51 Mustang, the P-38 was credited with destroying more Japanese aircraft than any other USAF fighter. With a distinctive twin engine design and the nickname 'the fork-tailed devil,' the P-38 was used on missions of photoreconnaissance and dive-bombing. The closest Wally ever came to flying one happened as a mere fluke prompted by generosity. A couple of nights after his flight with the American captain, Wally left Del Tahquitz Bar and heard a short moan coming from the bushes. He commandeered the help of the bartender to lift whatever was moaning out of the bushes. It just so happened to be Wally's squadron leader. Wally asked the bartender if he could get him a spare room where his boss could sleep it off. He did and the two of them poured the commander into bed.

Two days later, Wally was asked to go and see his flight boss. The commander asked if everything was alright and didn't mention anything about the other night. Wally mentioned that he was hoping to get into P-38 transition and that it was a dream of his to fly one. The commander told Wally he would see what he could do. The next day Wally was ordered to come to the flight line for P-38 transition. He would have to check out in a B-25 first and then get a couple of hours flying the Douglas A-20, and then he would be ready to fly the P-38.

The call to war would come before Wally got a chance to pilot the P-38, and he would be forced to give up that particular dream. Wally was able to arrange for a week's leave before heading to war, but was now in need of a ride to Odessa. He went to the flight line office where he was lucky enough to find an Officer heading to Odessa/Midland in his radar P-38. The P-38 was a single-seat plane, so Wally would have to ride in the cramped, barely ventilated, tremendously hot, nose/radar compartment. Wally was more than welcome to come along he was told, and he even convinced the pilot to buzz his house when they got to Odessa with a high-speed fly by. Using a water tower where Wally had painted his name in large black letters as a child, he directed the pilot to his childhood home. Wally had phoned his family from Tucson where they had stopped for fuel, so his entire family came running out of the house when they heard the P-38. They were in the backyard just in time to see the plane roar by at treetop height.

After a quick visit with his family, Wally returned to Palm Springs the same way he got there, but in a different airplane. He bummed a ride in an AT-6 from Midland Airpark. When he got back to Palm Springs, chaos had broken loose. Operation Overload was in full effect, and, when Paris was liberated on August 25, 1944, it was evident that the war was reaching a major turning point. Throughout August and September of 1944, Wally participated in several evacuation flights, taking wounded soldiers from the Pacific back east and vice versa. On October 18, 1944, Wally was assigned to a C-47 to be ferried from Bangor, Maine, onto Goose Bay, Labrador, and across the North Atlantic to Reykjavik, Iceland. From Iceland, he would proceed to Scotland, then London, and he was finally transferred to an Air Transport group based at Le Bourget in Paris.

Duty at Le Bourget airdrome in Paris was the next enviable location for a young aviator to be based. Charles A. Lindbergh landed at Le Bourget after the world's first solo, trans-oceanic flight, and seventeen years later Wally was stationed there. Being at Le Bourget also meant proximity to the German lines. Wally was less than 200 miles from the action, which meant the situation could become life threatening at any moment. Every flight Wally made from then on was further complicated by the thought of death hanging over him. But, the Germans were giving up ground after the fall of

Paris, and, in just five months, they would be in full retreat with the entire free world pursuing them.

Wally's duties while based at Le Bourget included delivering supplies to airdromes near the front lines and taking the wounded over to England. As Operation Overload and the breakout from Normandy allowed Allied troops to advance towards Germany faster than anticipated, an initial lack of deep water ports and the incredible speed at which the Allies were gaining ground created enormous supply problems. Wally found himself aiding ground troops in an effort to contain the fighting to German soil and stall Hitler's chances to launch an offensive.

Convinced that his armies would be able to defend Germany in the long-term if they could just neutralize the Western Front in the short-term, Hitler launched the Ardennes-Alsace Campaign, known generally as the Battle of the Bulge. Put into action on December 16, 1944, the Battle of the Bulge was an unsuccessful attempt to split the American and British Allied lines in half. The plan was to capture Antwerp, Belgium, and then proceed to encircle and destroy four Allied armies, forcing the Western Allies to negotiate a peace treaty in favor of the Axis powers. Around Christmas of 1944, Wally was sent to Marseille, France, to pick up fresh troops and deliver them to the front lines for an Allied counter offensive in the now heated Battle of the Bulge.

War and Bravado

Wallace Scott, Personal Journal, June 25, 1995

"Hitler was rapidly approaching a state of madness, yet still looked upon himself as the greatest general of all time; even greater than Napoleon. In recent weeks, he became desperate. It was desperation without hope. He had to do something to lift his people back to their old plateau of glory. He confessed to his first blunder for penalizing Field Marshal Gerd von Rundstedt, supreme Nazi commander in the west, who had not been able to successfully follow his Fuehrer's own military orders. He has replaced von Rundstedt with General von Kluge. When Kluge failed Marshal Walther von Modi, who fared no better, replaced him.

"Defeat had followed defeat for the German high command, and they had only one place to crawl, back to the most brilliant general at their disposal, von Rundstedt, and von Rundstedt almost turned the whole affair around. Just inches kept him from blasting all the way back to the English Channel. His tanks ran out of fuel just short of the American fuel dumps, which he – von Rundstedt –was aiming for. It would give him all the fuel he would need.

"No! He could not have won the war, or even come close, but he could have reinstated the Germans their pride, if only he had not met the resistance of a band of Americans at the Battle of the Bulge. The Germans were fighting doggedly all along the front, as they were pushed back onto

61

their supposedly impenetrable Siegfried line. No one had done this to them for hundreds of years. The Germans were temporarily helped by the weather that allowed them to operate without the fear of our air power.

"They took advantage of this and our fighting men along the breakout called the Bulge were in dire need of fresh troops. These new men were to be in Marseille, and we were to send hundreds of troop carriers to pick them up for delivery to the front lines. It seemed that all the C-47s in France and England were to converge on Marseille on Christmas Eve in order to deliver the fresh recruits as near to the front lines as possible. On the flight down from Paris, lights were prohibited and radio chatter was incredibly dangerous. It was very dark and miserably cold. We made the trip with a few mid-air, near misses, but didn't lose a single plane. We made it to Marseille and set in for the night. The incline of the metal floor caused me to not only be freezing, but to come out from under my blankets which had to be rearranged at least a dozen times. I thought about the boys in the foxholes, freezing in the mud, no lights, no heat and the German infantry crawling around in search of them.

"The next day I couldn't wait for our troops to come aboard so that I could start the engines and get some heat going. The troops that came on board were as young as or younger than I was at only twenty years of age. I talked with a couple of them, and of course I wished them all the best. They too had that look in their eyes, not bravery or lack of bravery, not eagerness, but a fear of the unknown. We delivered these boys to the front lines of Marseille, delivering what may have been fresh cannon fodder for the Germans. The realization of the suffering that was taking place on the ground, the men fighting in harsh elements and getting frozen feet, was the driving factor for many of us more fortunate ones flying around in heated airplanes to be doing what we could to aide them. In an airplane, I was allowed the comfort of at least an imagined detachment from the realities of war.

"During one flight in particular I was confronted with the reality that we were in fact flying during a war. My co-pilot, Pete, and I had been commissioned to fly supplies from Paris to General Anthony C. McAuliffe's men in Bastogne during the Battle of the Bulge. It was early January of

1945 and incredibly foggy. The C-47 we had been issued was the same ship I had flown over from Nashville, and I knew its condition was far from perfect. We would be flying blind in poor weather without any help from radio navigational aids. We taxied across the frozen mud at Le Bourget. Once we had taken off, we immediately got on top of the now solid undercast. Pete and I were very cautious with our headings and flight time to our destinations. We would soon be starting our descent for arrival at our destination, or hopefully somewhere very nearby. We started our descent and did not break out of the soup until we were only 100 or so feet from the ground. We were surrounded by slag piles poking skyward into the soup.

"'Keep your eyes forward Pete and your nose glued to the windshield,' I said. 'If you see something coming, do whatever is necessary to miss it, including taking over the controls. I will not fight you. This may call for a lot of teamwork. I'll keep my eyes forward for a few minutes. You look around for distinguishing landmarks. We've got to find ourselves.'

"We were dodging the tailings piles that were several hundred feet in elevation and with our near zero visibility we didn't have much time to dodge them. We finally found a river and decided to follow it north to the nearest town. We eventually came to a good-sized town where there was a lot of wartime activity taking place. I even saw what appeared to be a red-cross ambulance. This must be friendly territory we thought. We continued up the river to the north, still at a very low altitude, and the country was taking on a lowlands look. Finally, I saw one, a huge Dutch windmill. This had to be enemy territory. I started to make a wide turn back to the south. Then it happened. We were under fire. Sounds of enemy anti-aircraft fire kept coming from buildings, barns, haystacks, patches of trees and any other kind of concealment. They were sprouting long streams of fire and it was all aimed at us.

"I pushed the controls forward to the firewall and at the same time jammed the mixture, props, and throttles to the forward limits. Pete got up to start shooting the colors of the day, thinking we might be taking friendly fire, but he didn't know the colors and neither did I. We surely didn't have time to look them up. 'Shoot any color Pete; just keep shooting that Very pistol until all the flares are gone. They may think they are shooting us and pieces are coming off. Keep shooting!'

"We were buzzing at treetop height at full power, due west. There must have been a hundred German 88s firing at us, and the only reason they didn't hit us was our low altitude. Evidently, they couldn't track their guns fast enough to keep us in sight, and shells would not explode at such a low altitude. We were still headed west and hopefully toward friendly territory, when we saw another airplane. It was a pursuit ship, and it was coming in for a landing. Pete and I couldn't tell if it was friend or foe aircraft until another one dropped out of the clouds, and we could see it was an English Hurricane. We went in for a landing following the Hurricane and were met by a British officer wanting to know what we wanted, where we were going, and where we had been.

"We answered his questions, and we were admonished for flying in such dangerous territory. Then the officer pointed us in the direction of McAuliffe's men. We reached them without further mishap, and they were glad to finally see us. Their own situation was still very tenuous. They desperately wanted for us to take a planeload of wounded back to Paris. I hesitated, telling them about the worsening weather, predicted heavy snow storms, and told them about the trouble we had with the aircraft. 'The way it has been going it might act up again at any moment. You can order me to evacuate a planeload of troops, and I will be glad to comply, but the way our luck has been going today, I hope you don't.' I told them.

"The officers decided not to risk it. Pete and I climbed back aboard our fateful C-47 and prepared ourselves for the flight back. We taxied to the end of the runway, and everything seemed to check out. We had a slight crosswind from the left, so I didn't notice the malfunction right away. It was necessary to feed slightly more left throttle to offset the effect of the crosswind. It didn't help, I fed in more left throttle and it became necessary to start applying right wheel brake. Even with nearly full left throttle, we were veering to the left. Glancing down at the manifold pressure gauge, I saw that we were almost at idle power for the left engine.

"I brought the C-47 to a stop and went to check what was wrong. Eventually, we shifted to high blower to see if the low altitude blower was out. It was and the left engine produced near normal power on the good high blower. Now we only had one blower to each engine which meant if either failed or malfunctioned it would be necessary to continue the flight on one engine. We did not even consider spending the night in Bastogne. Marshal von Rundstedt and his elite S.S. Corps were thought to be out in the woods, and an attack was imminent. Pete and I glanced at the instrument panel many times in the next few hours of flight, and we were very thankful things happened the way they had.

"After take-off and before we had gone ten miles, the weather socked in right on down to the deck. It started snowing. We started climbing and the higher it got the colder it became. Icing became a problem. The snow was wet and the flakes looked like ping- pong balls. Finally, at an altitude nearing 10,000 feet we broke into the clear. It was nearly blinding, as we were flying into a lowering winter sun. We started scanning the skies for aircraft, but if we did see an airplane we could always hide in the clouds we were skimming across.

"Time passed, and it was time to bite the bullet. No radios. No beams or other navigational aids. We were on our own. Paris must be near, only scant miles ahead we hoped. We started our descent and were losing altitude as rapidly as possible. The snow was still heavy, negating any forward visibility, and we wanted out of these skies as soon as possible. We really didn't slow our descent until down to about 2,000 feet above sea level, remembering that the Eiffel Tower was nearly 1,500 feet above sea level. We descended even more until we were only a couple of hundred feet over ground elevation. Nothing but pure whiteness stared us in the face until we were nearly snow blind.

"'We're going to have to go lower Pete! Put your forehead against your side window and look straight down,' I said. 'When you see anything, let me know immediately. We will level off at that altitude. Our time is up for being over Le Bourget, so I am heading north and we will box the area until we recognize something. Anything!'

"In another moment Pete said he saw something, and I dipped the right wingtip so I could look. I saw it too. It was a large estate home close to Le Bourget and about the right distance away for base leg. 'Pete do you recognize that house? It is nearly in the flight pattern of Le Bourget. I am starting my turn to the final approach heading and will descend another hundred feet. Yell out if you seen anything, and turn the windshield wipers on full speed and give them an extra shot of alcohol. This has got to be it.' We got below minimums, and Pete reminded me of the taller buildings around the airport, but then he said, 'runway dead ahead. Wheels down and locked.'

I yelled for full flaps and cowl flaps to go to trail. 'Thank god we made it,' I said. We sat there in silence. We didn't have to say a word. Each knew what the other was thinking. This was an impossible day, yet here we were with everything intact and none the worse for wear and tear, except for maybe a few frayed nerves and a couple of completely useless super chargers. I entered this fact into the flight logs, and stated also that the aircraft should be inspected for shrapnel damage. 'Shrapnel damage?' an officer would ask later. 'What exactly did you guys get into?'

Dum Dum

The Battle of the Bulge became the single biggest and bloodiest battle that American forces experienced in World War II, with over 19,000 men killed. But the planned German offensive was halted, and the German forces were left severely depleted of men and equipment, while the Allied troops continued to gain ground on Germany. In February of 1945, within two weeks of Wally's return to Paris from Bastogne, he was transferred to Dum Dum Airfield on the northeastern edge of Calcutta, India, and away from the front lines. Dum Dum was very near to Headquarters at Hastings Mills in Calcutta, and it served as a major supply point for ferrying supplies to Generalissimo Chiang Kai-Shek's forces in Kunming, China. This was known as 'flying the hump' for its proximity to the Himalayan Mountains.

The move involved a complete weather change from the freezing temperatures in Paris. Wally made good use of his time in India and even managed to travel to Egypt to see the Great Pyramids. He spent eleven months enveloped in mosquito netting with plenty of bug bombs of DDT sleeping in a tent with three other men. On his flights, he found the mountains between India and China to be high and treacherous. Altitudes were so great that the storms, winds, and icing would make these routes the most dangerous in the world. For the Allied flight crews, flying over the hump proved to be a nearly suicidal endeavor. The planes were often overloaded and very few of the large supply planes were fit to be flying through the Himalayas. Appropriately nicknamed the 'flying coffin', the C-

46s were often returned to the factory for extensive modifications and corrections of mechanical problems.

Wally began flying in India before the monsoon season started. The absolute worst weather would be over the Chindwin hills. The hills are a weather trap and trigger precipitation mechanisms for all moisture-laden winds coming off the Bay of Bengal and the Indian Ocean. These winds would be lifted by the Chindwins and condensed into very large cloud formations reaching into the stratosphere. The moisture would be squeezed out in the form of rain so heavy it could drown out an aircraft engine. During the monsoon months it became necessary to bypass the Chindwins, which meant flying through the Brahmaputra River Valley a better, though not by much, weather option. He flew C-47s and C-46s, and he was able to fly to the upper reaches of the Brahmaputra River Valley without having to detour over the Chindwin hills.

Scotty came through Dum Dum on his way back to the United States. He had been flying combat time, which counted for time and a half. Scotty was able to return home after 750 hours accrued airtime, whereas Wally would spend a total of fifteen months overseas. He eventually acquired enough instrument time flying the Brahmaputra River Valley to become captain and carry large passenger and cargo loads. Flying secret cargo missions made the trips incredibly dangerous, especially when even he didn't know what he was carrying.

Chiang Kai-shek

Wallace Scott, Personal Journal, August 5, 1995

"I felt a little suspicious as I stood outside Major Jimmy Martin's office waiting to be briefed on my next flight from Dum Dum. I stood in the hallway, my eighteen-year-old frame hidden under my ATS uniform, and anticipated my next flight. Normally I would report to operations to pick up my orders, check on the weather, and then head to the flight line to go about the rather mundane duties of repetitious flying. About the only thing that ever changed was the weather, but typically not the routines. Today was different.

"Soon I was called in by Major Martin and into an office tinged with a mysterious aura. I had the distinct impression that the operations officers were attempting to downplay my next assignment. 'Sergeant Scott, you will be taking a special shipment to Chabua. There you will either be further briefed at Chabua or off-loaded for your return flight to Dum Dum,' Major Jimmy Martin stated.

"I was then told that my load, while not being very bulky, was extremely heavy; no attempts should be made to reposition it. 'Sergeant Scott,' the Major continued, 'you are to make certain that no one fools around with this load. If at any time you are asked what you are carrying, you are to reply that you do not know,' which was very true. I had absolutely no idea what I would be transporting. I explained to Major

Martin that I understood my assignment and left without further questions.

"During our take-off from Dum Dum, it became apparent that we had been overloaded and that the aircraft had been 'weighted and balanced' improperly. My co-pilot, another man named Pete, and I were flying with a very tail-heavy distribution of the load. My curiosity as to what was weighing us down hadn't been particularly piqued up to this point, but I was starting to get interested.

"The first point on our flight from Dum Dum to Chabua would be at the north side of the boarder of Bangladesh in the district of Lalmonirhat, popularly called Lal-Hat, which was 239 miles away at a heading of 18 degrees north. If you were to overfly this airport by less than thirty miles you would be in very tall mountains, in the height range of 20- to 29,000 feet. From Lal-Hat, we would continue onto Tezpur, which was 221 miles away at a heading of 74 degrees east. The terrain just past Tezpur consisted of mountains reaching from up to 15- to 20,000 feet. We would be flying 'up the valley' at altitudes as low as 5,000 feet. This mandated a slight turn to the right in order to stay in the valley. It was very important to locate this turn point; luckily, Tezpur had a very good rotating beacon that could be seen from over one hundred miles away, weather permitting.

"Assuming we made it to Tezpur, our next point would be Jorhat, which sat eighty-seven miles almost due east (88 degrees) from Tezpur. The valley was constricted through here. You were not only close to the Himalayas both dead ahead from you and off to the north, but the Chindwin Hills were alarmingly close on the right side. From memory, I would guess the valley to be less than twenty miles wide. Finally, the trip from Jorhat to Chabua would be the last seventy-eight miles at a heading of 49 degrees to the northeast. The total distance from Dum Dum to Chabua was 625 miles and normally took around four hours, figuring a true air speed of near 160 mph. A light or empty load could make you slightly faster. My speed on this flight would be decidedly slower due to the overload and imbalance of the aircraft.

"Just as twilight was upon us, Pete and I were on our way. It did not take long on the flight to Chabua to realize it would be a memorable one. The weather, which was predicted to be bad, became steadily worse as the flight drew on. I decided to remain below cloud base at around 5,000 feet in order to remain as close to visual flight rules as possible. The heaviness in the tail of the ship was making it difficult to fly the C-47. I was becoming more and more concerned with the poor response to our maneuvering in the rough air. After about an hour and a half of trying to keep the ship as level as possible, I decided we needed to do something about it. I had been told not to loosen the heavy load, so when we came within radio range of Lal-Hat I gave them a call.

"The static electricity was surprisingly manageable and Lal-Hat answered our call right away. I requested that they allow us to come in and land for a redistribution of our load. I informed them that we were so off balance that we could only maintain a cruising air speed of 110 to 120 mph. We were told to stand by and wait for a decision. Pete and I exchanged worried glances. I could tell he was as certain as I was that landing was unavoidable. After what seemed like an eternity, Lal-Hat answered our call: permission to land had been refused. That was it. No reason given.

"I appealed their decision, assuring them that the plane and cargo were in jeopardy. I told them that if the weather became more turbulent and, if we had to fight any harder to maintain control, Pete and I were in danger as well. Once again, we were told to stand by. I thought back to my training, the extensive amount of time we spent learning the mantra 'safety comes first', and I decided to tell Lal-Hat that I was starting my descent. A response came back to me, 'Negative, do not land under any circumstances. You are directed to continue your flight as filed. Repeat! Continue with your flight. Do not land at this station.'

"I gave them a Roger and began to look around for enemy aircraft. That must be it; the danger must lie in a threat from other aircraft. Why else were we being treated like this? A safety call had been refused, but why? Could our load really be so important that landing would be that high risk? I was suddenly fascinated by our important load.

"As we proceeded down this leg of the river valley, we were in visual contact with the ground and could see the river often enough to comfort our fears. Above us solid overcast hung just a few feet from the aircraft. The moonlight, if any, would've been covered by the thick cloud blanket. Fortunately however, there was no rain, and we could see the beacon light signaling our turning point at Tezpur.

"Chatter that sounded like two truckers conversing about enemy aircraft came over the radio. There was something about bogies and enemy aircraft sightings near Tezpur and Jorhat. I had seen them, even in the daylight, but the enemy wanted nothing to do with my lowly C-47. I returned my focus to the ground below us, the only view we had, and continued to listen to the two buddies chatting. Suddenly a dark apparition appeared dead ahead, crossing from right to left. In the stormy weather, it appeared as nothing more than a large shadow, but it soon became apparent that a two engine aircraft was staring us in the face. We had extinguished our lights just as this bogie had, and the two dark shadows lingered in the air together.

"I immediately called Tezpur, gave them our approximate location, and told them about our bogies. They informed us that the bogies had been in the area for the last forty-five minutes, and that they had not caused any problems as of yet. Knowing that just because they hadn't didn't mean they wouldn't, I continued onto Chabua wondering if the enemy aircraft wanted whatever it was I had on board.

"The more gas we burned the more tail heavy the C-47 became. I was flying with 50% forward (nose down) trim on the elevators and anticipated a tricky landing. I knew I would have to keep up speed for control purposes, but with the nose trim setting down this far it could be interesting. Pete and I talked about our upcoming landing and decided to come in on a two-mile final in our 'cruise' configuration. We would have to keep close to our cruising speed in order to have elevator control. The plan was to fly the ship onto the ground and immediately start applying wheel brakes in order to keep the tail in the air. The slower we went, the more necessary the wheel brakes would become until we lost most of our lift in the wings.

"It all went as planned until it became obvious that the excessive speed and weight in the tail were going to put us at the very end of the runway before we could stop. The brakes were fading fast because of the heat build-up from the speed. The end of the runway felt as if it was sliding towards our nose. We kept on the brakes and prepared for a sharp and fast turn onto the taxiway. The turn was suddenly upon us; we put our full weight into the brakes and braced for the turn. With one wheel hitting the ground off the taxiway for a brief moment, we made the turn into Chabua.

"The operations officer informed us that the load would be taken from us here, and that it would be picked up by another plane. I was relieved to get rid of this load. I told them to be careful on the weight and balance and got ready to turn around and get back to Dum Dum. We would return to Dum Dum empty, thank God. It would be almost 15 hours for the trip, or a total of 25 hours before another chance to crawl into my bed.

"By the time we returned to the C-47, our mysterious load was gone. We climbed into the empty plane and headed down the runway. The return flight to Dum Dum was uneventful. The night felt cooler than usual in Dum Dum. The fires of nature that feed the monsoon storms were laid to rest for yet another day. The weather was beautiful all the way back. The stars had taken their place back in a rain cleansed sky, and they now seemed so close you could reach out your hand for them.

"We arrived back at Dum Dum, and I immediately headed to the de-briefing officer. This was the customary thing to do, and for this flight I had questions that needed to be answered. I felt someone owed me an explanation for the ridiculous weight[1] and balance of the aircraft I had just flown. I desperately needed to know what was in that load. I said these very words to the de-briefing officer who then exchanged a glance with another

---

[1] Note: Approximately $10 million in gold would have been about 17,000 pounds at the 1945 price of gold.

officer who said, 'It won't hurt to tell him now. You were carrying ten million dollars in gold bullion for Chiang Kai-shek. We're not certain, but we were told that it is a loan.'

"'Loan my foot.' I answered. 'I'll bet it was a gift. If I had known, I would have flown off somewhere and retired.' I said this with a smile and rather pleased with myself that I had just been in the presence of such a 'loan.' 'Well that explains the weight,' I said and prepared to make final comments on the flight. When the job was finished, I headed directly to my bed where I would finally get to sleep for at least 8 hours then I would get up, and there would be another flight awaiting me."

India Hogyah

Wally's goal was to make it home by Christmas. After his trip to Chabua, he asked to be put back on regular status where he would get more flying time and be able to get out sooner. After the Axis powers surrendered and the Japanese followed suit, World War II would finally end on V-J Day, August 15, 1945, but it would take several more months for Wally to complete the 1,000 hours that were necessary to fulfill his duty time. He made every flight possible, flying again to Chabua, Madras, Colombo, and always back to Dum Dum. He was promoted to Flight Operations Officer, which meant more duties on the ground, but he would not let that stop him from flying.

As he approached 995 hours of flight time, Wally began to look into getting on an airplane that would take him back to the states. He requested a seat on a flight that would get him to New York December 18, but it was full. He checked into flights that would put him in on December 22nd or 23rd. Both turned out to be full as well. He finally found a flight leaving on December 16th that would have him in New York City by his deadline of December 24th. They gave him passage for it, but requested travel orders saying that he had completed his time. Wally told the scheduler that he didn't have them quite yet, but that he would have the required hours by tomorrow. They gave him until noon the following day. He had to beg, borrow and threaten to get his travel orders, and eventually the Major gave into the holiday spirit and cut Wally his orders for the next morning. In the meantime, Wally had to schedule a flight that night to make sure he would get his 1,000 hours. His remark in his logbook after this last flight was 'India Hogyah' which loosely translates to 'Gone from India.'

On December 16, 1945, at 21:00, Wally climbed aboard a C-54 four-engine airplane and headed home. He would ultimately fly through Barrackpore, Karachi, and Habbiniya in India and then onto Baghdad, Rome, Prague, Brussels, London, the Azores and Newfoundland before he finally landed in New York City at 17:00 on December 24th. He did it! He'd made it home by Christmas. Once back in the states, Wally first and foremost craved fresh milk, a luxury that was near impossible to obtain while in India. Next, he and the boys wanted steak, but roamed the streets of New York to find everything closed for the holidays. Their first meal stateside would ironically be Chinese food. As they wandered around, a group of girls passing by looked at them and culled, 'hubba, hubba.' The boys looked at each other and decided this must be a new slang term they had missed while overseas. One of the boys yelled 'hubba, hubba' back. The girls turned around. The guys had won the right to take the girls out for a drink, and the rest of the night was spent readjusting to being home.

Wally left New York City on December 26th aboard a train headed for Dallas. He had called his mother in Odessa from Rome a few days before, and he would head to Odessa as soon as he had checked in at Dallas Love Field for final orders. After spending a few days at Love Field and flying some solo time entitling him to his pay for another month, Wally went home to Odessa. He returned to a life that would never be the same again, and to his family who remained just as he had left them fifteen months ago. With new prospects and a world full of opportunity on the horizon, Wally was relieved to be finished with his time in the military, and he began to settle back into Texas.

1931 Wally Scott, age 7, growing up in Iraan, TX

1944 Wallace Scott in England during World War II

1942 with family; left to right Winnie (sister), Don Duckering and wife Agnes (sister), Scotty (brother) with his wife Francis, Wally at age 18

1944 Nashville, TN. US Army Air corps officer training. Wally in front row

Wally in England, World War II   Wallace and Scotty

On leave in Egypt Wally on camel in center

1952 Wally and Boots

1952 Twins Dema and Deby, 1 year-old

1956 Wally at archery range, Odessa TX. Before taking up soaring, both Wally and Boots were accomplished archery sportsman. In 1959, Wally became Texas State Field Archery Champion.

Wally with radio controlled model glider in their yard in Odessa, TX

Wally in Schleicher Ka 6 CR

In Schweizer 1-26 over hangars at the North end of Odessa-Schlemeyer airport

Boots and Wally Jr. before her first glider ride with Wallace as her pilot

PART 2 - THE SECOND LEG: 1946 - 1974

We Meet for a Good life

Boots Scott Interview Odessa, TX June 16, 2005

'Wallace tells it differently,' Boots said, 'his version's slightly more scandalous than mine.' She sat up a little taller on her sofa, happy to be at the point in the story where love meets Wally Scott. At seventy-eight years old, Boots looked like nothing but a slightly older version of her 18-year-old self in the wedding picture I hold in my hands.

When she was born, Boots went nameless for the first six months of her life. Her father wanted to name her Dessie May after his mother, while Boots' mother wanted to name her Beverly. In the meantime, her grandmother had begun calling her Boots from the *Puss in Boots* cartoon character in the weekly 'funnies.' Boots was finally given the name Beverly May, but by this time the name Boots had stuck. At barely eighteen years old, Boots had been working as a bookkeeper at the bank in Odessa and living with her aunt and cousin since she left her hometown of Council Hill, Oklahoma, several months before she met Wally.

Wally had been in Odessa for a few months working at the theater and helping out where he could. The 1,000 hours he had just spent flying overseas had exhausted his desire to be in the air. So he stayed earth-bound for awhile, reacquainting himself with Odessa and picking up new interests. He began an active social life filled with the dances and the general cavorting he associated with his hometown.

On a particularly warm evening in January of 1946, Wally and the gang headed out to the Ace of Clubs for a night of dancing. The girl he had been seeing since being home and some other friends had taken a table on the far right side of the club. On the left side of the room and more towards the bar Wally's future wife, Boots, sat at a table with a boy named Bobby Greer. Bobby, a blind date, and Boots were accompanied by Boot's cousin Mary Joyce Parkes. From what Boots had to say about the first time she met Wally, it was love at first sight.

'The first time I saw Wallace he was on the dance floor in full uniform. He was dancing with a girl he was going with at the time, and he was just back home from the war. I told my cousin that he looked like a good dancer, and that I'd like to dance with him. Mary said, 'You wouldn't like him, he's too arrogant.' Bobby overheard me say this, but Bobby didn't dance. So he went over and got Wallace, who happened to be a schoolmate of his, and introduced me. Then, he asked me to dance. We started out on the dance floor. I remember exactly what I had on. It was one of those low-waisted dresses with the full circular skirts. It was black crepe, and it had a great big wide ribbon around the waist with a big bow and little cap sleeves. He took my hand and started to step down to help me off. He turned to me and said, 'Hubba, hubba.' I turned right back at him and said, 'Well hubba, hubba yourself big boy.' In Wallace's version, I threw my arms back and put my chest out when I said this, but I just don't remember doing that."

Boots and Wally started dating and would marry quickly. Running from Wally's mother, who wasn't quite prepared for the marriage, the two kids eloped to Carlsbad and were married on May 12, 1946. After some time, they gained Maggie Scott's approval and eventually moved back in with her. Wally began taking classes at a local college and working nights at the Scott Rio Theater, while Boots maintained their new home under the watchful eye of the other Mrs. Scott. Wally and Boots continued to live with Maggie for another six months before moving into a home of their own.

The first of four children, Seree, was born in December of 1947, after a year and a half of marriage. Wally Jr., nicknamed 'Wally Whoa' by Seree, arrived in February of 1950, and twin girls, Dema and Deby, followed the next year. Wally continued work at the Scott Rio Theater during the five years they had four children. In 1951, the Scott family opened The Plains, a new drive-in movie theater. Wally moved from working at the Scott Rio Theater to managing The Plains at night.

Around the same time Wally started managing The Plains, he picked up a new hobby: archery. His brother, Scotty was an avid bow hunter and got Wally interested in the sport. Wally set up targets at the drive-in and began shooting archery at night. There was also a club in Odessa with a shooting range. Targets were set up all over the club. Most had animals on them, and the brothers would practice shooting all the time. 'It got to be a pretty big thing here,' Boots remembers. Wally became very involved in the sport and eventually went to the Texas State Championships.

Never one to miss out on a good time with Wally, Boots herself was soon hooked as well. The two of them began shooting all the time. 'We were glued,' she said. 'Whatever he did I did. I worked three days a week at the Scott Rio Theater doing books, and in our spare time we would shoot. We relied on one another.' Boots and Wally took the kids to Corpus Christi, and Wally shot. Then they went to San Antonio to shoot. Then they went to Houston to shoot some more.

In 1956, as president of the Permian Basin Archery Club, Wally won the highest score of any instinctive archer in the National Field Archery Association's Championship Tournament in San Antonio. One of two types of aiming, instinctive archery does not involve pins on the side of a bow to be adjusted for distance as sight shooting does. Three years later, Boots placed second in the state tournament in Odessa, and Wally and Boots took home the husband and wife team trophy. This trophy now sits in the display case in the dining room. A picture of Boots and Wally with bows in hand rests beside the trophy.

It was right before the yearly trip to the state tournament in 1961 that Wally decided to forego the trip to stay and fly power planes. Wally had let his military flying license lapse, needing a break from flying after the war. A precocious six-year-old Wally Jr., who had become intrigued with flying machines, goaded Wally into renewing his civilian pilot's license. He started flying here and there while he was shooting archery, but it took years before it again became a passion.

Archery had been taking up a great deal of his free time, and flying was time-consuming as well. 'And, you can't do both,' Boots explained. 'So, we made a decision.' Wally focused his attention on flying. His hours at The Plains drive-in restricted him mostly at night, which meant he could fly during the day. He soon spent several hours flying every day he could, and he began instructing Wally Jr. at a very early age.

Taking his children up in the Piper Super Cruiser that Wally eventually bought was just one of the ways the family became involved in his flying. Wally Jr. writes of his first flight with his father, 'Once I was up in the air, my dad told me that I could unbuckle and stand up so I could see out the window. I stared down on the earth below and knew that this is where I wanted to spend my life...in airplanes and flying above the earth. Thank you for this, Dad!' Wally Jr. was the most flying-centric of the children. When Wally Jr. was in sixth grade, he once forgot to pick up the girl he was to go on his first real date with because he was so involved flying a U-controlled model airplane with his dad the afternoon of the date.

What was once a childhood ambition and a wartime asset would soon become a lifestyle that involved the whole family. In 1961, at the age of 36, Wally would soon find there was an aspect to flying that he hadn't discovered yet: the art of gliding. 'I didn't know how I would fit into soaring until we got the glider,' Boots said. 'When we got it, it was covered in soot. It was in this wooden shipping crate having arrived via train straight from the manufacturer, and we took it out to the airport, all four kids and I, and it took forever to clean all the soot off. I found out then what I'd be doing!'

Sailplanes and Soaring

Wallace Scott, Personal Journal, October, 1961

"On March 20, 1961, I had just finished a beautiful afternoon flight in my four place power plane when I ran into Roy Schlemeyer at the Ector County Airport. Within a few minutes of conversation, I learned that Roy had recently retired and now found himself busier than he'd ever been while working. The reason, I was surprised to find, was soaring. After being introduced and becoming enchanted with soaring, Roy and another pilot, Al Parker, decided to open a rather informal soaring school. They now found themselves overwhelmed with interested students and spent at least half of every day in the air.

"I had seen sailplanes, also known as gliders, occasionally when they flew off from here and remembered experimenting with engineless flight in my J-2 Cub. But, other than that, I cussed the sailplanes that got in my way, just as any good power plane pilot would do. Roy told me that Al was up with a student in the 2-22 right now. 'Would you like to come and take a free flight?' Roy asked. 'OK,' I answered, never one to miss an opportunity to fly something new, especially when free. Roy introduced me to Al after he landed and was finished with his student. Al took me on a tour of the aircraft, explaining this and that, and then he strapped me into the front seat. The next move was something I had witnessed before, but always got a chuckle out of. Roy took his Buick automobile out onto the runway and drove it to one end of the tow-line opposite the glider at the other end. The

Buick and the sailplane were then hooked onto the line. Once the traffic was cleared off the runway, Roy started slowly driving down the runway taking up the slack in the line with the Buick. Once the line was taut, the Buick began to pull the glider down the runway. We were off to a very rapid and abrupt climb out. With one jerky motion, the glider sped down the runway with me in the front wondering how we'd ever actually make it into the air. At about 35 mph, I felt the wind catch beneath the wings of the glider and slowly we left the runway and ascended into the air.

"At about 800 feet, we disconnected from the tow-line and made a short circuit of the field with me following along at the controls. The flying part of the glider ride felt natural and smooth, only slightly disarming that there was no engine to rely on. We spent some time flying straight and level before coming in for a landing. On the ground, Al took a few minutes explaining other aspects of soaring and told me that I could follow him through on the controls for the next climb out. Another tow was made with Roy's steadfast Buick, and the ship was under my control after release, up to and even including the landing. 'Would you like to make one more?' Al offered after we landed. 'Sure,' I said, and off we went. This would be the last flight of the day.

"Al and Roy were operating again when I got to the airport the next day, and I watched from the big hangar. I noticed things I had not noticed before. I saw the sun glisten off the tow-line and noted how smooth the sailplane was in flight. I made my way down to the guys to say hello and found myself once again in the sailplane. After this ride, I was asked if I wanted to just go ahead and get checked out. 'How long will that take?' I asked. 'You could probably solo this afternoon,' Roy replied. It was just too easy to say no. I made the next take-off and pattern. Al inferred from my progress that I had been thinking about this overnight. After two more circuits and two simulated line breaks, Al stepped out, and I took the 2-22 around solo.

"The next day I was out again. I was rechecked in dual before Al let me take it up again solo. The wind had shifted slightly, and I was asked to land on another runway after the circuit. Roy towed me off, and I soon noticed that I was in "up" air. I worked it rather easily and gained to 6,000 feet MSL, or 3,000 feet above ground. Now this was fun. After forty or so minutes in the air, I looked down to the airport and saw people waiting for their turn to fly, so I came down.

"'Why'd you land?' they all asked me on the ground. 'When you can soar on a day like this, go ahead and soar. Don't worry about the man on the ground.' But, I had had my fun for the day and was ready to let someone else have a go. The fellow that was waiting was a guy I had known for several years that I flew with overseas, Red Wright. 'Are you a sailplane pilot?' I asked Red and found that he was new at it, but he was already passionate about soaring. Red flew the 2-22 up to the other end of the field and, after we put the ship in the hangar, we all went out for coffee. This was to be the first of many discussions over coffee that would be the place to compare, learn, put over theories, set theoretical records, boast, razz and have a generally good time.

"The day after I made my second solo flight in the 2-22, I made an appointment to meet Al and Roy at the field the next morning to get checked out in the 1-26, a one-design class, single-seat sailplane that would soon become a personal passion. I helped walk the ship down to the other end of the field, about a mile and a half, and with Al's last minute instructions in mind, took the 1-26 for a few trips around the field. This ship flies beautifully; it was much easier to boss around than the 2-22. There were no thermals and I couldn't gain any altitude. But, I knew that the 1-26 would be a wonderful machine to fly. After we put the ship up that day, we all went again for coffee. The conversation during this lull in activities again turned to the 'whys' and 'hows' of soaring.

"These coffee breaks turned out to be sort of a personal ground school for me. I learned as much here as I did in the air. It seemed that nearly everything that presented a problem could be figured out or diagrammed with a pencil and paper. I was eager to learn. I had a good and varied background in flying, but I was always surprised how much a person could learn by listening and asking a few questions along the way. If no one happened to know the answer, as was often the case, we would figure the problem out amongst us.

"I made it out to the airport nearly everyday. Roy, Al and Red were often around and served as a continual guide. I soon ordered a ready to go Schweizer 1-26B, which was manufactured in 1961 and cost around $2,150. The bug had officially bit. The next bite would come from the competitive soaring bug, but, in the meantime, I would make small advances in my new 1-26."

Cross-Country

Once Wally began flying seriously, he quit shooting archery almost completely and retired his bows to the garage. He spent his days at the airport and was at The Plains drive-in theater at night. Boots and the kids would join him often at the drive-in. Boots would make beds in the back of the car. Even in the winter, she would set up heaters and go to the drive-in. The kids would make burgers on the theater grill in the back of the snack bar and sell snow cones while standing on milk crates during intermission.

At Christmastime, Wally would dress up like Santa and often the kids would be awoken to a, 'Ho! Ho! Ho!' bellowing out of the air-conditioning ducts. In the summers, Wally and Boots would take vacations with the kids around the country teaching them to water ski and snow ski and to drive boats, cars and go-karts. At Halloween, Wally would sit on the roof dressed in black and swing sheets down on hapless trick-or-treaters as they approached the front door of the house. Some years he put himself in a coffin in the front yard and would rise up as kids approached. Always a jokester, the kids inherited Wally's sense of humor and stick prickly grass burrs on the back of his pants whenever they got the chance. During the fall, winter and spring, while the kids were at school and Boots was busy doing books for the Scott Rio Theater, Wally went soaring. Alone in the cockpit, Wally worked on his technique and honed new skills for the strong condition, upcoming summer soaring season.

Seated in a tight cockpit, Wally learned to look for areas of warmer air that push the glider up into the air. Called thermals, they are invisible columns of rising warm air caused by solar radiation. The sun warms the ground, which warms the air above it. This warm air becomes lighter and wants to rise, but the cold air around it wants to sink, creating an unstable equilibrium that forms a bubble of hot air near the ground. Once a catalyst or trigger, such as two cars passing or a farmer mowing, encounters this bubble, the warm air begins to rise and creates a thermal in the air. A cu, the abbreviation for cumulus cloud, is often associated with a thermal and will sit on the top of the thermal. With a steady wind, cumulus clouds can align in rows, or cloud streets lining up in the wind direction. As Wally learned about lift (rising air) and glide ratio (feet of forward distance traveled compared to feet of altitude lost), his soaring abilities progressed dramatically. A 'good soaring day' called for heat from the sun and some instability in the air mass to trigger thermals which, if enough moisture is present in the atmosphere, can form cumulus clouds, thus giving away the location of the thermals.

When in the glider for hours at a time Wally, would find that it could best be described as, as friend Marion Griffith put it, 'Well you're hot.' Wally would learn to cope with this and other physical challenges as his flights gained in distance and the minutes inside a cockpit became hours. Though it feels like one would get bored after 6 hours in a glider, as pilot Jim Callaway notes, 'It seems like time stands still. When it's over you think, good Lord I flew for 6 hours, it sure didn't seem like that.' The concentration required and the flow that comes from being engaged the entire time makes the time fly by. 'You're making a decision every second for 6 hours,' Sherman Griffith says. 'A modern analogy would be my sons' ability to play a video game for 6 hours straight,' Mark Huffstutler adds. 'Once you're at cloud base, you're constantly mentally and physically engaged in this.' When up in the glider, Wally's focus was entirely on the horizon. Fighting to find the next thermal, he pushed himself to stay up just a little longer and go a little further. He was constantly trying to read mother nature to determine his next move.

Between April 2nd and May 25th of 1961, Wally accomplished his Silver

'C' badge set by the Federation Aeronautique Internationale (FAI) and regulated by the Soaring Society of America (SSA). The Silver 'C' is the first in a line of badges acknowledging internationally recognized levels of soaring achievement. It is obtained through three required elements: a 1,000 meter altitude gain above an in-flight low point, a flight of five hours duration after a tow release, and a distance flight of fifty km (31.07-mile) cross-country.

On April 2, Wally gained an altitude of 1,500 meters above his in-flight low-point. The next day he conquered the distance requirement on a flight from Odessa to the Monahans airport and back for a total of thirty-nine miles. But, the flight did not qualify for the Silver 'C' because there was no barograph on board to record the flight's time and altitude progress, one of the rules set by the Soaring Society of America. On April 15th, Wally flew from Odessa to Crane, Texas a distance of 35.5 miles. This flight was recognized by the SSA. Finally, to complete the Silver badge, Wally flew from Odessa to Big Spring to Sterling City then to Barnhart to Mentone and finally Tankersley to surpass the five-hour duration requirement while getting in some cross country flying practice.

During the spring and summer of 1961, Wally flew cross-country to Wellman (78 miles), Morton (122 miles) and Haskill (182 miles). Late that summer, Wally reached an altitude of 4,000 feet above the low-point to complete the Gold "C" altitude requirement. The following summer in June of 1962, Wally would reach the Diamond badge level in all the required elements.

As it began to control his days, Wally slowly began to learn about weather and was soon forced to learn the weather charts and forecasting as well. As his knowledge grew and his soaring skills steadily improved, Wally became more competitive about the sport. Keeping track of previously set records, Wally focused his cross-country flights on breaking free distance records.

Breaking the Distance

Adapted from: Wallace Scott, "443.5 Miles by 1-26 N8606R"

Soaring Magazine, October 1963

"My ambition in the last year and a half has been to beat the 1-26 distance record of 373 miles set by Helmut Roemer, a German soaring pilot, flying out of Albuquerque, New Mexico. Last August, a year ago in 1962, I had a very enjoyable flight for my distance Diamond in a 06R following a dog-leg course from Odessa to Plains, Texas, to Roswell, New Mexico, and on to Tucumcari, New Mexico, for a total of 330 miles. This has been a terrible year locally for distance flying, but, regardless of this fact, an encampment was planned for the first two weeks in August. A gathering of the clan was scheduled for the flying to be attempted from either here (Odessa) or the Marfa-Alpine airport, halfway between Marfa and Alpine, Texas.

"Some of our good friends arrived a week or so early, including Ben Greene from North Carolina and the John Randalls from Florida. The time was spent flying locally, and bemoaning the poor weather for this time of year. John tried bravely in his new Sisu 1A for some distance flights, but they were all aborted. Ben couldn't be talked into any exploratory flights in his new Standard Austria. Al Parker ended up with John's Sisu, and, low and behold, August 1st loomed as a good cross-country day. Some of the boys were already at Marfa, but the ones here decided to go cross-country that day out of Odessa. I took the first aero tow at about 10:10 a.m. and left the airport confines about fifteen minutes later with 2,000 feet in hand, after working up from a low 900 feet after tow.

"The first half hour was a struggle, but about seven hours and twenty minutes later I had completed one of my most enjoyable flights yet, 380 miles in total distance. This was a three-legged, dog-leg course, with turn points at Hobbs, New Mexico, and Tucumcari, New Mexico. This beat the 373-mile record as far as I knew, but I was disappointed when I landed and measured the distance as 350 miles. The next day, back in Odessa, you can imagine my elation when an accurate re-measure of the flight showed 380 miles.

"I had successfully beaten the 1-26 record by a mere seven miles, and I was thirsty for more. I missed an exceptionally good day on August 5th when I aborted an eleven a.m. tow, thinking it would be too late in the morning. This turned out to be a very good day, and I was in contact with Ben Greene and Red Wright by radio as they came zooming up from Marfa with fantastic air speeds reaching 85 mph. That night my weather man advised me that August 6th would be a repeat of this day, and I was ready for another flight.

"The next morning found me at the airport with my son at 9:00 a.m. We got the 1-26 out and on the line, and as I was laying out the car tow-line, my wife drove up to act as tow pilot in our Buick. "At 9:30 a.m. I was in the air on the first attempt, where I found zero-sink lift, but soon lost it and landed. My next attempt was steady sink. Cu's were not predicted until eleven I made the third attempt immediately and found 50- to 100-fpm (feet per minute) lift that soon fizzled. I delayed my fourth car tow until 10:05 and cut loose at 900 feet in lift. I worked it for twenty minutes to 2,300 feet above ground and said goodbye once again to Odessa. I had declared turn points at Lovington, NM, and Clayton, NM, with the hopes of landing in Scott City, Kansas. The slight wind, about 5 to 10 mph, had drifted me too far north of my course line, so I had to set in a slight crab, clicking along at 55 mph. My next thermal saved my flight, 900 feet above ground, but I was able to work it up to about 3,000 feet. Down again to 1,000 feet at five miles south of Frankel City, but was saved again by cu forming nearby. Now the left was getting better and began to form cu's,

102

and I set off for Hobbs and Lovington, increasing the indicated air speed. Near Hobbs, I was up to 9,000 feet MSL in 500-fpm lift under large cu's. Now the day was really beginning to boom.

"Over Hobbs at noon with seventy-five miles stowed away, I wouldn't work lift for the next hour unless it was better than 500 fpm. I expected the lift to weaken over the farming area south of Clovis. It did, and I had to be content with 500 and 1,000 foot climbs in the area. The next fifty miles or so were a nightmare. The clouds were there, but they were just hanging motionless. They weren't working at all. They weren't moving across the ground at all. I found myself working lift I had decided against one minute, and flying back to a moment later.

"I was about ready to abort and go to Dalhart, where my family was to await word from me. I could see Dalhart on the horizon, and I was tempted. One fair thermal enabled me to head for Nara Visa where the clouds looked better, and they were. Off to the race again. Now I could work 5-, 6- and 700-fpm lift to my next turn point at Clayton. After taking three photos of Clayton, I struck out on a heading of thirty degrees to a large cu about ten miles out. There was a large, cloudless hole toward Kansas so I gave up my goal. I had to detour about ten miles east to pick up the only likely looking cu within reach. I soon had a steady 500 fpm, then stronger and stronger as the cloud was pulsing itself anew once again. I then saw something coming from under the small clouds. I realized a line squall from a storm was coming hell-bent in my direction.

"The wind was wedging under and rolling up the dust. I had to get on the ground and soon. Should I land at Springfield? No, I thought to myself, only another 380-mile straight-line flight. I would go as far as I could to improve my straight-line distance. The line squall was moving rapidly, and it was over Lamar now, which gave me no option of landing there. I was at 85 miles per hour on the airspeed and refusing good lift. Then at red line and burning off the altitude. Where should I land? I will need help. Maybe I can land on the lee side of some farmhouse, or a grove of trees. No, I needed a more substantial offering of help and a firm place to tie to. I have seen these fronts whip up winds to sixty or seventy mph. Then I saw it, my landing spot. On the highway, there was a service station with a large services apron. Clear the traffic on the highway. What about the truck I passed a few minutes ago? Yes, he is far enough back now. I wait for two cars coming from the north to pass and down I go telling myself to watch for that mailbox. I land it fast and hot, full brake, screaming tire, off the highway and slinging gravel until the wing touches down five feet from the Ethel pump.

"I hopped out of the glider to find the dogs going crazy and the owner and his wife looking slack-jawed. I started shouting orders to bring a hammer for the driving of the stakes. I pointed the nose of the glider into the wind and tied the ropes to both a big steel sign and to the release hook. Then I drove in the stakes for the wings and tail. With the help of a man who had just driven up, I tied the plane down with nylon ropes from my kit and pulled the spoilers and the break to tie them on as well. I grabbed the camera and barograph from the glider, in case everything else blew away. Then the wind hit, but my Schweizer 1-26 N8606R was snug and rode the winds beautifully. This complete tie down operation took about ten minutes. The wind blew for twenty or thirty minutes and then it began to rain. I introduced myself to the people that helped me. Then, I desperately needed a coke and a cigarette. I tried to relax a little, but found it difficult to do so. My family was on their way from Dalhart to where I was near Clayton and now the worst part of the day lay ahead of me. The hours of waiting and worrying about them on the highway were far more nerve-racking than any time spent in the glider. I think about them while I'm flying when I'm not forced to concentrate on other things. I find myself saying, 'Just protect them, will You?'

"This flight managed to be a total of 443.5 miles for the dog-leg distance. I took off at 10:05 and landed at 18:39 Central. A braver person could have taken a ride on the cold front that made me land, and I'll never know how much further I could have made it that day. The country is beautiful from up there, but in one minute it can look pretty grim. To me, this is a pretty great sport of ours. The thrill of the hunt, the chase, cool breezes in your face at high altitudes and the sweat of the furnace room stoker at low altitudes. Tranquility, desperation, tranquility. Fun? You bet.

Rooftop Tradition

With this flight on August 6, 1963, Wally set a new distance record with 443.5 miles. He flew from Odessa to Lovington, New Mexico, to Clayton, New Mexico, and started on his way back in eight hours and thirty minutes. In a typical general aviation power plane, 443.5 miles would have taken less than four hours, Wally's eight and a half hour flight was starting to become the average amount of time he would spend in the air while on cross-country flights.

Gliding is a solo pursuit. However, Wally's family soon found out that the competitive side of soaring would involve the entire family. In what he writes were many of the happiest hours of his life, Wally spent much of 1961 through 1964 in his 1-26. On weekends and, whenever possible, on weekday afternoons, the Scott family drove cross-country in pursuit of Wally. Boots remembers they'd wake up on a spring or summer morning and never knew quite where they'd be that evening.

The young family was an eager crew in the beginning. Boots began leaving a bag by the front door of the house with overnight clothes, snacks and games ready for a last minute departure. In the fall of 1963, another tradition began. Wally would wake up early in the morning, climb onto the roof of their house and look south toward Marfa. If the cu's started to form, Wally would claim it a good day to fly and head to the airport.

With a growing family and its inherent expenses, all of Wally's soaring was on a budget. Aero tows at $3.00 a pop were too expensive, so Wally stuck with car tows and Boots' role as Wally's car tow pilot became solidified. The Buick Century station wagon would end up making hundreds of car tows in its 100,000+ mile life of service. Boots would come out to the airport from work and, still in high heels, she would hook Wally in his 1-26 to the towline then drive to the end of the line, hook up the Buick, make sure airport traffic was clear and rapidly pull the glider into the air. Once Wally was all the way up, he would release the line. Boots would then unhook the Buick, stow the tow rope, get back in the car and return to work. For as many weekends and weekdays as she can remember when she wasn't working, Boots would take Wally to the airport, tow him into the air and then go home to pick up the kids and get on the road heading in the same direction Wally was set to fly.

The road trips were exciting for the car full of Scott children. Crossword puzzles and chewing gum in hand, they would entertain each other on the long trips. Some road-trips involved staying at a hotel, which meant only one thing to the kids' a swimming pool. In the days before their budget allowed for radios and good instruments, Wally and Boots used the Scott Rio Theater as a switchboard to stay in touch with each other on the road. Every couple of hours or whenever he was able to, Wally would radio the nearest airport and tell them his location. He would then have the airport call the theater and give them his details. When she could, Boots would stop at a pay phone and call in to the theater to get Wally's information. Often a couple of hours and a couple hundred miles off, at first Boots had a difficult time keeping track of Wally as his course changed with weather. Over the years however, she became an expert at reading the weather and figuring out what impact it might be having on Wally's flight path.

On a flight northwest to Arizona many years into distance gliding, Boots showed up at Wally's hotel only a few short hours after he had arrived, a difficult feat for a car chasing a glider. Boots went immediately to the desk clerk and asked for the key to her husband's room. She snuck up to room 108 and put the key in the door. The door caught on the security chain after it opened a few inches. Hearing the door open, Wally yelled out, 'Who the hell is that?' He unlatched the chain and jumped back at the sight of his wife. 'Surprise,' Boots said, thrilled to impress her carefully calculating husband. 'I had you at least two more hours behind me," he exclaimed.

Wally Jr. began crewing for Wally. Everyday after school, he would go to the airport to help his dad as he landed. If he was lucky, he got to go up and fly. Wally was a tough, military-like teacher and flight instructor to his son. After his teaching experience with all the cadets at Fort Stockton, Wally had zero tolerance for mistakes. This, however, is what Wally Jr. credits for making him a safe and skilled pilot. Wally Jr. soloed at fifteen in a sailplane and sixteen in a power plane, the earliest the FAA will allow for soloing power-planes, but he probably could have soloed at twelve with the training his father provided while flying in their power plane prior to 1961. He would go on to set 12 Texas junior class, senior class and open class state soaring records, and he would eventually compete in several regional and national soaring competitions.

With Wally Jr.'s help, Wally began preparing for his first major soaring competition, the 31st Annual National Soaring Championships, which was held from June 29th to July 9th of 1964 in McCook, Nebraska. After three years of purely focusing on distance flying and with a new distance record under his belt, at the age of 40 it was time for Wally to experience the other side of soaring; competition. These are two different soaring disciplines, requiring different mindsets. There is some overlap, of course, and many pilots will try both. But, for the most part, glider pilots tend to be better at one or the other. George Moffat for example will always be remembered for flying competitively, and Wally Scott will be remembered for flying straight-out distance. Nevertheless, Wally would fly competitions for 30+ years. Wally did not like being told when and where to soar, which is why the competitions would always be secondary to him. Despite this, he would prove to be a talented competition pilot. Wally's first ever competition would be an indication of exactly that.

The 31st Annual Soaring Championship was organized by six soaring enthusiasts from McCook, Nebraska and held at the old Army Air Base located eight miles northwest of the town. The largest turnout since 1947, the forty-eight sailplanes assembled represented the 'cream of the country's motorless aircraft crop.'[2] Making their debut appearance in the competitive world, two BG-12s and one Zugvogel III made the display of sailplanes all the more extravagant.

The local papers noted newcomer Wally Scott and his 5th place finish on the first day of competition. Flying a Ka-6 in weather that was described as 'unpredictable' at best, Wally would continue to impress the competition when, on the third day, he soared at an amazing 49.91 mph average speed keeping close to the faster Sisu gliders that lead the competition. On the sixth contest day, the task was a 212.5-mile triangle in which Wally was one of only nineteen pilots to make it to the second turnpoint. In a streak that kept getting better, Wally tied for the second best flight on the seventh contest day. By the ninth and final day, Wally finished fourth for the day, but second overall. With a runner-up finish in his first National meet, the August 1964 edition of Soaring Magazine reported the pilots to watch in the future and gave an entire passage to Wally, stating: 'They are young, talented, and knowledgeable pilots and will be strong threats in the future. Without doubt, the most amazing performance was by Wally Scott placing second in his first major competition.'

---

[2] Soaring Magazine, August 1964

The Growing Expert

Wallace Scott, Excerpt from a 1963 speech to glider pilots in Hobbs, NM

"Since my first glider ride two years ago in March of 1961, I have logged well over 3,000 hours in sailplanes, flown 21,000 miles of actual cross-country, and flown nearly 600 hours cross-country. Last summer, after waiting for the big weather day, I decided to lower my demands and fly on a day that was only looking mildly successful. I took a chance and achieved a near 600-mile flight to McCook, Nebraska.

"For days on end, the weather patterns north of us had been stagnated with a stationary front lying across Kansas. Then one morning, on the *Today* Show, the cold front was plotted to be backing up as a warm front and was running due north along the 103rd meridian (longitude). The moisture content of the air was good, and by flying to the north, by keeping out on the west side of the warm front, I thought I might possibly get far enough to the north for a good flight. But then, after a last check on the *Today* show, I called flight service to see what the morning winds and sky conditions were along the intended flight path. The actual conditions to the north of Amarillo and through Kansas were very dismal.

"Record low temperatures, solid overcasts, and quite a bit of fog and rain appeared to be facing me. I decided to fly locally, and the local weather remained good. The next morning, the *Today* show showed the same frontal conditions exactly, as the warm front was shown to be in the same place. My call to flight service gave the same dismal reports coming out of the stations to the north.

"The next day, the *Today* show again repeated their favorable flying predictions, but again the flight service had bad reports to the north. Even worse, in fact, as the weather bureau showed the long stagnant cold front to be further to the south in the Amarillo area with predicted heavy rains and turbulent weather. Well, talk about feeling it in your bones, I knew they had to be wrong. Boots and I went to the airport at about 8:30 a.m. and got everything prepared. Shortly thereafter, Marion Griffith from Dallas drove up pulling his large Nimbus 2 sailplane. We told him that we were making a try to the north and offered to help him put his Open Class ship together. But, as he had also checked with weather personnel, Marion reckoned he would wait until tomorrow. I told him that I knew they were wrong and that tomorrow might be too late. He looked at me with a questioning glance and then offered an excuse of not being totally prepared and said that his family was still at the Motel.

"Boots and I continued with our preparations, and soon I was in the air. The day turned out to be weak until I was nearly into Kansas, but then things got good quickly. The warm front rapidly moved to the east, leaving strong southerly winds in its wake. The flight was a breeze later in the day. In northern Kansas, I called the McCook airport Unicom on the radio and talked with a few glider friends there and was persuaded into pulling on the dive brakes from 10,000 feet and spiraling down to visit with people I hadn't seen in years. At the time, I knew I was throwing away many, many additional miles of good soaring weather. I landed there at 6:00 in the evening. The sky ahead was beautiful. In retrospect, I know I passed up 100 and perhaps even 200 more miles, but the instinct I felt about the day had been correct, and my flight had taken me to a place I wouldn't have gotten had I passed up this day.

"I guess what I'm trying to say with this story is that there is no way I could stand up here in front of you for one hour, or ten hours, or ten years and tell you how to fly cross-country. You've got to get out there and do it, and make mistakes and make yourself a storehouse of knowledge. You've got to make things happen."

Making Things Happen

On July 23, 1964, a year after his McCook flight landed him amongst friends and also fresh from his first National Soaring Championships, Wally set his first world gliding goal record in his Ka-6. On a goal flight from Odessa to Goodland, Kansas and with a distance of 520.5 miles, Wally set a new FAI world record and broke the current distance record of 487.24 miles set by fellow Odessan Al Parker. A goal flight includes a predetermined landing site declared prior to take-off. The pilot must land at the declared site for the flight to count, making it that much more difficult. The Al Parker that Wally beat was the same guy that introduced Wally to soaring and who took him up for his first glider ride just three years ago. Gliding in 1964 was a small, friendly sport loaded with neighborly competition, especially in Odessa. Famous worldwide for its soaring weather, Odessa is a hot spot for sailplanes, and many gliding records have at one time or another been set on a flight out of Odessa. Wally moved into new territory with this record setting goal-flight. But, by the end of 1964, Al Parker would beat Wally's new record with a 647.17-mile flight.

However, his record flight would still gain Wally the distinction of being the only man in the world to hold both a world archery and world soaring record. He was quickly becoming one of the top glider pilots in the world. The next year confirmed this status when he was selected for the 1965 World Gliding Championships in South Cerney, England, as part of the U.S. Soaring Team.

113

The first World Gliding Championships took place in Germany in 1937. With the world at war, it was eleven years before the pilots resumed competition of a peaceful nature. The Championships have been held every two years since 1948 (except in two instances where there was a three-year break.) A competition as much about aircraft as piloting, the Germans, Brits and French dominated the top for many years. Nevertheless, the Americans produced four world champions; Doug Jacobs (1985), George B. Moffat Jr. (1970 & 1974), A.J. Smith (1968) and Paul McCready Jr. (1956)

At midnight on May 18, 1965, Wally and Wally Jr. boarded a TWA Boeing 707 flight to Mildenhall, England, accompanied by team members Ben Greene and J.C. "Red" Wright. The first team the Americans came into contact with was the South Africans, who they immediately befriended. On the other hand, the U.S.S.R. team seemed 'quite disconsolate,' at first, but proved to be strong, superb athletes. As Red Wright remembers, 'On the coldest days when we were shivering from the cold and all bundled up in extra clothing, they were wearing open sandals, short-sleeved shirts and Veretennikov would be sporting his ever-present hair net, which simply proves my theory that a good jolt of vodka is a prime training stimuli for whatever.'

Whereas the weather was surprisingly beautiful for the competition in England, for the Americans it was reminiscent of cool, bad weather by Texas soaring standards. To navigate the countryside, the U.S. Soaring Team relied on an incompetent crew car driver. The entire gang remembers a few close calls on the winding roads to Lasham. The driver was a chap by the name of Dennis, a local with a Ford Zodiac who Wally had hired to drive the team during the competition. Dennis claimed knowledge of the roads came from years of local driving experience, and then he got lost forthwith. Red Wright described him as having the feel of a 'frustrated Grand Prix driver.'

The arrival of Prince Phillip brought excitement one rainy day, but mostly the hubbub of the competition was the sailplanes. The exotic and different sailplanes participating in the competition bridged the language barrier and kept the competition respectful and entirely enjoyable. Some of the world's first high-performance, fiberglass reinforced, plastic sailplanes appeared at this competition. With new gliders like the Glasflügel H-201 Standard Libelle, the eventual paradigm shift away from metal and wood construction to fiberglass for sailplanes had begun.

Flying a Ka-6 CR, Wally credited his success in England partly to Wally Jr., who crewed for him. Wally finished sixth at the World Championships—the best finish by an American pilot ever to that date. Due to his achievements at the World Championships and for his flying record up to this point, Wally was inducted into the Helms Soaring Hall of Fame, later to become the US Soaring Hall of Fame, in 1965. While Wally competed at the Worlds, Boots stayed at home with their other three children and ran The Plains drive-in.

Wally and Wally Jr. returned home beaming with success and all smiles. The entire Scott household headed into the summer of 1965 with the wind beneath their wings, so to speak; Wally would soon head out to his next national soaring contest in Adrian, Michigan, Wally Jr. would take up soaring himself and make his first solo flight during a rest day at the Adrian soaring contest, and the twins would head into high school in the fall.

MOJO

The 32nd U.S. Nationals in 1965 were held in Adrian, Michigan, so, after returning from England, Wally had a short two-months of training at home in Odessa before he drove to Michigan. He would place tenth overall in what was only his third soaring contest ever. The rest of the summer would find Wally at the airport during the days flying cross-country and working the drive-in at night.

After only a couple of years of cross-country trips, the girls grew tired of them. It wasn't as much fun as they thought at first. The swimming pool didn't entertain them like it used to, and being in the car for hours on end was boring. As they got older, Boots had to stay at home, and the job of launching, driving and crewing fell to Wally Jr. The twins, Dema and Deby, were cheerleaders at Bonham Junior High School, and Seree was a cheerleader at Permian High School, home of the famed Permian High School multiple state championship football team. The book *Friday Night Lights,* which became a movie in 2004 and a TV show in 2006, is based on the Permian Panthers and their mascot 'MOJO.' In Odessa, the Permian Panthers were, and still remain, the obsession of the town in large part because of the general rivalry between the blue collar Odessa and the white collar Midland not too far away. It always gave the Odessans a great amount of pride to beat Midland Lee High School, and they very often did just that.

Over the next several years when Wally wasn't involved in soaring or working, he was home with his house full of MOJO teenagers. The Scott family attended every MOJO Permian Panthers football game there was. Both Wally and Boots were avid fans, and their kids were just as involved.

Wallace and Boots Scott were known for their victory parties. Every Permian Panthers win was celebrated with a band playing in the garage and dancing and food for the kids. The 20-gallon cooler used at these parties still sits in the garage, although it has been years since it was full of Orange Crush. The large backyard would be filled with the team's players, parents and a highly committed fan base. Coach Mayfield, the Permian football coach at the time, was known to stop by and join in the festivities.

This being Texas, there was nothing bigger than football. With three daughters as cheerleaders, the house saw a constant stream of school-spirited activities. The Scott household was rarely without a football or basketball player hanging around, most likely courting Seree, Dema or Deby. Even after the kids were out of school, Boots was known to patch up uniforms, and Wally won a Permian Spirit award in 1971 for his commitment to the Permian Panthers. In his later years, it would be flying and 'MOJO' that got Wally going in the morning. MOJO the battle cry of the Panthers means simply 'Go like hell.'

The downtown Scott Theater, a new addition to the family's corporation and built in 1959, became the host to many of the kids' high-school birthday parties. They would invite friends to watch a late-night movie and, once the customers all left, Wally would 'sleep' in his office and let the kids have the run of the place. They'd turn the music up loud, have coke cup wars and create a huge mess. On one occasion at Wally Jr.'s birthday party, a few boys locked themselves in the custodian closet and wouldn't come out. All in good fun, Wally shot his pocket size, tear gas cartridge pen gun under the door within seconds the boys came pouring out of the closet. Boots recalled how no one seemed to get any sleep at those parties. Mandatory clean-up of the theatre by everyone began at 6 a.m.; this was the rule for the kids to have more parties there.

Wally had his summer days to pursue gliding. In the summer of 1966, he participated in the 33rd U.S. Nationals in Reno, Nevada, where he again finished tenth overall, but had an impressive second place finish in the standard class, which is a category of sailplanes with 15-meter wing span and no flaps. That same summer, Wally set a state speed record in a sailplane at 62 mph on a triangle flight from Odessa, to Snyder, to San Angelo, Texas and return.

The 34th National Soaring Championships was marked by long flights during the day and camaraderie at night. Wally's family was the best crew a pilot could hope for. Every good crewmember knows how to tow a trailer, understands hand signals, fix parachute straps, wax the glider and make sure the pilot is fed before take-off. The more experienced crew, however, knows how to find an out-landing field in a hurry, how to carry the glider out of a corn field and how to take apart a glider in 40-mph winds. Boots and Wally Jr. especially were the most experienced of crewmembers and the rest of the family would fill in as necessary.

The airport and local motels played host to dinner parties for 'glider guiders' that lasted well into the night. Over the years, the pilot's wives often became the best of friends, sharing and participating in all aspects of soaring. On the bustling championship days, it was the wives and children of the pilots that ran the show. Before launch, they were on the runway helping their pilots get ready and, after everyone was up and flying, they sat on the sidelines with folding chairs in the blistering heat, waiting. Once the sailplanes were on course, there were hours on the ground when it was just the crews and families. They would go to retrieve their pilot, if they landed out or await their return to the airport. For the crews, this part of the Championships was mostly a waiting game.

The Championships, however, were few and far between. The majority of Wally's flying was in pursuit of distance, and, therefore, the carefully calculated business of record flying would develop as his forte.

Soaring Game

Adapted from: Wallace Scott, "The Preparation and Execution of Long-Distance Flights" Soaring Magazine, June 1982

"Why cross-country and why record flying? I thought I would open this article with some of my views on these questions. Why cross-country? The most obvious response is that a soaring pilot has to go cross-country to obtain his Silver Badge, then to get his Gold Badge, and then some more in order to get his Diamond Badge Goal and Distance Legs. Another answer would be that a glider pilot, with any adventure in his bones, will not long be content to 'flag-pole sit' over the airport.

"Why record flying? This is not so easy to answer. We have to start at the very beginning, even before we go cross-country. Man, by his very nature, is competitive. This surfaces in us glider pilots soon after we solo. Just let another glider show up in your thermal and you will instinctively try to compare your abilities with his. If he is able to out climb you, you might say something like, 'Maybe he knows something I don't know,' or maybe you might tell yourself, 'I've gotta work on this until I can stay up with that guy.' It won't be too long, however, until you are not satisfied to out climb just him. You'll find you're content only when you can out climb anybody who shows up.

"Now there are measures: A Silver Distance of thirty-one miles, or a Gold Distance of 187 miles, or the big one—the Diamond Distance of 311 miles. When they are conquered, what now can challenge you? How about a 500-mile flight or the 1000-km distance diploma? If your answer is yes, you have become a true long-distance lover and you start thinking, 'All this time, I have been striving to see if I measured up to prescribed goals of achievement,' and you will probably start pondering the ultimate challenge and measuring stick—world records.

"Of course, there are other ways to see if you measure up. There are the contests, all the way from local or club contests to the Regionals, then to the very highest, the Nationals. I would like to emphasize that I consider our Nationals to be the very best test of competitive skill. Our pilots are as good as any in the world, and everything being equal, probably better.

"Even in light of all this, I still think current world records are respectable enough to command equal or superior status to any National or World contest. To beat a current standard or world record, you are not just comparing a single day's flight with fifty or sixty other competitors—or even seven, eight or nine days of cumulative comparisons. Remember, a contest champion can win by the barest of margins, and he needs only to accumulate a few more points than the second and third place finishers. By comparison, a record-setting pilot is using as his standards the very best flight *ever* to be established, by anyone, anytime, anywhere in the world. His will become the ultimate measuring stick. That to me is the reason for 'why record flying?'

"So now, let's discuss records. Record flying is a very demanding, time-consuming, dedicated, and sometimes very costly aspect of this soaring game we love so much. You must do everything necessary to build your mind and body for an extreme experience. Many flights can tax your physical conditioning and mental acumen to the utmost, and even aborted attempts may call for more than eight hours in the air. If you're after one of the distance records, you had better be prepared for an eight and a half to ten-hour or even an eleven-hour flight. It is not unheard of for a pilot to lose ten pounds or more of body weight on one flight. The time is long past when you can venture out into the yard one fine morning, look up into the sky and think to yourself, 'This looks like a record day,' and then leisurely saunter to the airport and go about setting a new world record. You must start preparing yourself early in the season, long before the day arrives. If your record season is to last for one, two, or three months, you must be alert every day and night to those things you must watch for. This may mean fairly early to bed and definitely early to rise. It means much weather watching and predicting and many miles driven to the weather station to keep up with trends. You cannot prepare your body for a ten-hour sit with an occasional two or three-hour flight.

"I recommend taking early tows for practice in the weak morning lift, and this does not mean waiting for the cu to start popping, or to see what old Fred can do by waiting for him to take the first tow. You go first. Take-off a full hour or two before most people are even thinking about it. If, after take-off, the lift seems to be the least bit predictable, start venturing out on thirty, fifty or seventy-five-mile flights and start increasing the distances as the season and weather get progressively better.

"Start experimenting with the late evening lift, and try to make several flights whereby you land after sunset. It can be a beautiful time of flying, often with prodigious L/Ds (lift/drag ratio), and it is not hard to do on many days. Strive to log at least fifty hours and 2,500 miles cross-country every month. If you can do this for a month or two before your record attempt, you will be prepared. I know those figures will be hard to meet for weekend flyers, especially since weekends often have the worst weather. Just consider them as recommendations and adapt them to your own flying."

Master of the Barringer

The Scott household was quiet on the morning of August 23, 1967. Dema and Deby were now sixteen and heading into their junior year in high school. Lazy summer mornings kept them in their beds until Wally and Boots were off for the day. Today was to be a record setting day. After the World Championships two years ago, Wally began honing his record flying skills and now was working his way to being an 'old pro' of the sailplane community after a mere seven years in the sport. Wally had gained 18,000 feet for his Diamond Badge Altitude, the highest of the altitude category, just before he left for the World Championships in England in 1965, and he returned even more motivated to become one of soaring's elite.

In July of 1967, Wally would begin a long and rewarding relationship with a man named Barringer. Lewin B. Barringer, a former long-distance record holder and Soaring Society General Manager, stipulated in his will that a newly created Barringer trophy should be entrusted to the Soaring Society of America and be awarded to the person with the longest, straight-out soaring distance flight in a calendar year and not done at the US Nationals Championship. In place since 1948, the Barringer Trophy would become the premier soaring distance award. With the help of Wallace Scott, the Barringer would go from being simply *a* distance award to being *the* distance award.

A pilot must be careful to declare his flight appropriately for the distance to count. In many ways, the flight becomes an individual championship of sorts. The pilot picks the day, the time, and the course, but the event must be planned for well in advance and treated with the same regard as any major competition. One of the major differences between the two is that, with the Barringer distance, there is no limit on the number of attempts in a given calendar year. Thus, the trophy can change hands countless times a year right up to the last day of the year.

On any given day, glider pilots around the country are competing individually for the Barringer. On July 20th, 1967, Wally set out early in the morning, declared a distance record flight, and headed west toward Casa Grande, Arizona. After over eight hours in the air and 552 miles flown, Wally would hold the long-distance record so far that year. What did he do next? He set out to beat his own record.

The Roughest Hours

Adapted from: Wallace Scott, "The Second 500"
Soaring Magazine, November 1967

"Frank Shaw, the man we depended on for our weather in the Odessa area, had predicted that the winds from the east would stay that way all day. Day after day, Frank's forecast had been the same—poor weather for cross-country flying, but here on August 23, 1967, it looked as if his patience, and ours, was to be rewarded. My son Wally Jr. and I discussed the briefing that Frank had given us and decided that a flying day had finally arrived.

"First, however, a decision had to be made. Wally Jr. had his eye on Diamond distance. As for me, I had an unfulfilled yearning to make another distance flight to the west. There was some pretty formidable terrain in that direction, too formidable for an inexperienced youngster's cross-country flight (at least to my way of thinking.) Furthermore, I didn't want to use up one of the last good days of the year on a little thing like Diamond distance, so it was finally decided that I would take the Ka-6E for a journey to the west.

"Frank had told us that we could expect the first usable thermals between 11:00 and 11:30 a.m. As on several other mornings in the recent past, we put things in readiness for take-off and began the wait for the first signs of flyable weather.

"Wally Jr. closed the canopy, went to the far end of the line, cleared traffic, and at 11:50 a.m. we launched. Release was at 800 feet in a 200-fpm thermal. After a few minutes in this, I left to catch the southeast side of a developing cu over the north end of the airport. This one provided lift of nearly 300 fpm to 2,800 feet above the ground. These two little climbs took ten minutes, and, at high noon, the nose of the E was pointed toward the west and toward a promising sky.

"Progress to the next small cumulus cloud resulted in no loss of height. At the outset, I decided that there would be no rush, no maximum effort for speed. The flight would be leisurely. After all, I was flying with the sun, and my only real ambition was to make another 500-mile flight, so I went along flying fairly slowly, and with no low-altitude points. As I progressed, conditions slowly improved. My next thermal yielded 500-fpm lift; and from then, for quite a while, thermal strengths stayed between 300 and 500 fpm.

"The early part of the flight took the E and I just south of Kermit and on to a point about ten miles short of Orla. From here to the Guadalupe pass, the terrain is uninhabited, so I stayed as high as possible, from 3,000 to 4,000 feet above the ground to avoid any need to land in this area. Already, several small detours were necessary in order to keep in touch with the lift, but progress was constant, and by the time I passed south of Guadalupe Peak, I was 6,000 feet above the ground.

"Beyond the hills and into the salt desert, things got better. The clouds were now towering cumulus, and the average lift was near 650 fpm. The first lump in the day's pudding came about twenty miles north of El Paso just after crossing the Franklin Mountains. From here, I could see a large cu-nim to the north. It was raining heavily on the Las Cruces, NM area. The cloud just ahead was beginning to rain too, and, when I reached it, I was unable to find lift. It hurt, but the only prudent thing to do was to turn around and go back 20 miles to the mountains and lift.

"From here a detour was made to another large cu, one that did not start to rain when I got to it, but instead took me to a new high point over the desert. I could look down on extinct lava fields, extinct volcanoes, and a railroad track that ran off toward Deming, New Mexico. There was no other civilization for miles except for the Deming-Las Cruces highway far to the north.

"The cu's on course now were small, and elsewhere there was scattered overdevelopment. I contacted Deming Radio when I was fifteen miles southwest of that city and asked that a call be placed to my home reporting my position and the conditions. The operator came back on the air a few minutes later to inform me that the call had gone through and, at the same time, to advise me of a PIREP (Pilot Weather Report) concerning a storm twenty miles to the west of Deming. Perhaps, by now, it was dissipated, he said, but earlier hail had been so intense that the ground was white with it. As the cloud still looked active to me, I set my course a little more to the south.

"A final report from Deming Radio confirmed the over-development that I could see to the north and west. Toward Tucson, it was all darkness and cloud anvils, and ahead lay a large, rain-deadened area that meant a detour to the northwest. This took me to a point about ten miles north of Lordsburg, where I was forced to make yet another detour to the northwest. I contacted the storm area over high ground, and the E and I were now at our highest point yet, 13,500 feet above sea level.

"At this point, a decision on whether to continue toward Tucson, AZ or detour toward Globe had to be made. The former choice seemed the less formidable of the two, and a straight glide was initiated toward a large rain cloud over a desert dry lake. I went around the rain to the backside and found lift that got me to a new high of 14,000 feet MSL. Now, there followed a spell of gentle freezing rain that left a thin coat of rime ice on the wings and canopy. This shortly gave way to large raindrops and hail. From above, I could see millions of small white marbles cascading down on me. I slowed the E down, turned to the south, and was out of the area a moment later.

"I glanced back a few minutes later while working another thermal and saw the hailstorm now as a brilliant, white tapestry with a glowing aurora hanging from the cloud to the ground. It was beautiful, yet awesome, and it must have wreaked havoc on the life in the desert two miles below.

"I was back at 14,000 feet again and at the start of what appeared might be a successful final glide to Tucson. The overcast was solid now, and there were rainstorms over all the mountains. There was one patch of sunlight slanting down through the murk to the west of Tucson. It drew me on like a magnet. Severe areas of down associated with the rainstorms seemed the only thing that would keep the ship and I from our goal. There was some down as we threaded our way over the lower ground between the two large ranges of mountains, but this presently gave way to a five-minute climb in a 200-fpm thermal. Tucson was now in hand.

"I now informed Tucson Radio that Sailplane 2244 was about to land at International Airport – providing something could be done about the tower frequency, which I didn't have on my radio. They advised me to stay tuned to 123.6 MHz. When, ten minutes later, Tucson Radio inquired about my intentions, I was working another bit of 200-fpm lift that I'd encountered over Davis Monthan AFB. I now informed them that the flight might be continued. Would they please stand by?

"Tucson Radio now became curious enough about Sailplane 2244 to want to know what kind of airplane it was and whether or not it had an engine. It created a bit of a stir when I told them 2244 was a glider and powerless. They asked that I keep them advised, as they would undoubtedly have to make extra precautions under the circumstances. But, by now, I had seen some rising dust in the vicinity of Ryan Field and bid adieu to Tucson.

"Flying around a small shower, I headed for the dust and whatever turbulence there might be connected with it. My first contact with the lift, at 3,500 feet above the ground, was in the form of gusts. Then my hand, with index finger held lightly over the top of the stick, flew up and struck the canopy above my head. I was in the thick of it, gripping and choking the stick as if it were the only thing holding the E and me in the sky. I certainly had a thermal, but this was not thermal flying in the normal sense. One second the variometer would be pegged at 2,000-fpm up, the next at 2,000-fpm down.

"In this maelstrom, the speed had to be held at 65 to 70 knots in order to have adequate control. The barograph trace of the thirty-minute climb that followed shows it to be slow and erratic. Those big figures sound impressive, but I would have gladly swapped this monster thermal for a nice smooth one of only 200 fpm. The incessant gusts caused many quarter rolls, but gradually I got back up to 11,500 feet. After leaving this ragged thermal, I kept the airspeed low, near 70 knots, for fear of structural failure due to the sharp gusts. These were by far the roughest conditions I had ever encountered in my 1,400 hours of glider flying.

"It was growing dark as I approached Silver Bell, about midway between Tucson and Casa Grande. I had been in the air for nearly nine hours now, but it seemed just a short time. Just ahead was the edge of the shelf under which I had flown for some time, and seventy miles beyond that was the goal, Gila Bend. The last thing I wanted was a landing after dark in the middle of the desert. The decision, finally, was to head north toward Casa Grande. From here Gila Bend would be some 50 miles away and not too hard to reach, if I could stay high. Furthermore, there was dust in this area streaming out of the east, slowly arcing into the sky. Another storm was on it way.

"By the time I got to Casa Grande, I was down to 2,500 feet above the ground and searching, without success, for more lift. With my present altitude, I could progress another ten or fifteen miles toward the goal, but the storm was approaching rapidly now, and the prospect of landing in a dirt field with 40-mph winds approaching, and no one to help me secure the E, had little appeal. A call to the Three Point Airport brought an offer of help and an offer of hangarage for the night.

"That did it. I landed to the east on Three Point's taxi strip, rolled up to the hangar, and placed the tips of the E in the hands of four friendly people. I crawled out of the cock-pit, after nine hours and twenty-five minutes in the air, just as the first large drops of rain began to fall. Well, I missed the goal, but the story had a happy ending, anyhow. As it turned out, I did not use up the last good cross-country day of the year with my flight. Several days later, after the passage of a cold front, Wally Jr. took an auto tow and made a 325-mile goal flight to Perryington, Texas.

In retrospect, comparing this latest flight beyond 500 miles with my first one, I can find but one similarity. They were both pure thermaling flights, with no cloud street flying and with no long distances covered without loss of altitude. Although the second 500 did not deliver the thrill of the first, I did receive a note from Joe Lincoln (head of the Barringer trophy committee) that I'm extremely proud of. Joe wrote:

> 'I think your flight will do a great deal for the prestige of the Barringer Trophy. For some time this trophy has been taken for flights of modest performance, but now we have a situation where even a 500-mile flight (Joe's modest manner of referring to his own splendid flight) did not win it. I think this will have the effect of magnifying the prestige of this trophy into one of the great national awards.'

Encouragement like that makes you want to fly all the way to California.

King Kong vs. the Big Bad BS-1

Wally's second flight over 500 miles did not break his record from the previous month, and no one else would beat it by year-end. The 1967 Barringer Trophy was awarded to Wallace Scott. The next year, on August 5, 1968, he would win it again. With a flight of 492.2 miles to Oakley, Kansas, Wally would have his name engraved for the second time on the metal base of the gull-type sailplane wing mounted on the Barringer Trophy. Wally was officially the man to beat for long-distance flight recognition. Ready to defend his first-place Barringer position, he looked forward to next summer when he would attempt to beat not only the other pilots, but also, perhaps, his own previous records.

In addition to record flying during the summer of 1969, Wally decided to attend the 36th National Soaring Contest that was to be held in Marfa, Texas. Early in the morning on June 24, 1969, eighty-three sailplanes in four lines waited to be towed at the start of the competition. Australian, German, Swiss, Polish and other foreign languages mixed with Texan accents in the hustle and bustle of the runway activities. Four of the five available launching lines were in use and dozens of towropes were lined up just beyond the rows of sailplanes. The goal of the contest operations team was to get one sailplane launched every thirty seconds. Three world champions waited on the start grid.

Some pilots and crews sat shaded under the high-tilted wing of their ships. Others pilots scattered around the commotion and put on their parachutes while their crew clambered around trying to keep them shaded from the heat. The sound of revved tow-plane engines created a constant buzz. Adding to this were the voices of wing runners and the sound of tail skids scraping on the ramp during the take-off runs. Tow planes with sailplanes rose into the air at a brisk pace. Even running forty minutes behind schedule, the launch was unbelievably well-organized for a soaring competition of this size.

Bright red rags and water jugs were strewn out all over the runway waiting area as the last of the pilots got into their planes and gave a thumbs-up. The sound of the crews yelling commands back and forth over the tow-plane engine noise reached an almost frantic level, and then suddenly the intense activity was over. The sailplanes were all launched; the tow planes landed intermittently and headed into hangars. Disappearing into motor homes and hangars, the crews went to eat lunch.

The task of the first day of competition was a 262.5-mile speed triangle from Marfa to Van Horn to Fort Stockton and then back to Marfa. By eleven a.m. there was already thermal activity, a good sign since much of the terrain they would fly over that day was unlandable. On the leg back to Marfa, the pilots had to fly into a head wind the entire way. Wally followed the high ground. After hearing other pilots were having trouble with the wind, he took the high altitude to get home and had a straight glide to the finish line at 90 mph.

On day two, Wally had some trouble getting his first lift, but once again used what he heard from other pilots having trouble ahead to choose a slightly out-of-the-way but, ultimately, better course. Speeds of 100 to 105 mph won him the best flight of the day and put him in the overall contest lead. The competition had seemed to be what everyone expected with Ben Greene and George Moffat and Wally in the top three. But, word around the runway was that Wally and the high-performance ASW-12, which Wally had borrowed from Rudy Mozer, were going to be tougher than anticipated to beat. The Schleicher ASW-12 was one of the most controversial sailplanes on the market. While the Glasflügel's BS-1 was commonly referred to as the 'big bad BS-1,' the ASW-12 was known as

'King Kong'to both friends and enemies. Amid rumors that one of America's top sailplane pilots had taken delivery of an ASW-12 only to let in sit and gather dust, Rudy Mozer's ASW-12 made its first appearance in the hands of Wally. As Sherman Griffith remembers, 'This thing was a spaceship." It was the most feared, the most coveted, and the biggest advantage Wally Scott could imagine while competing in the Marfa U.S. Nationals.

The task for the third day was a speed task from Marfa to Van Horn and back for a total of 155 miles. The weather forecast called for cloudless waves of rising air from the east side of the higher ridges. Isolated thunderstorms were possible, but the contest meteorologist did not anticipate any wet weather. Wally Scott again made the best flight of the day.

On day four, Red Wright said of Wally, 'There are about eight months of soarable weather a year in Odessa. It is rare that Wally Scott ever misses a soaring day. He is probably the best-trained soaring pilot in the United States. If nobody else is soaring and there's no tow plane available, he'll get a car tow. He don't care if he only gets up to 500 feet on tow, he'll go on up. Today, he'll still be flying when the sun goes down.' A rough patch of weather at Rotan left Wally surrounded by rain. He escaped the cloud barriers by turning back and then heading south, but it cost him forty-five minutes and allowed Rudy Allemann to sneak up on him in the point standings, placing Allemann in second overall and a mere 4 points behind Wally.

After two mandatory rest days, the competition continued on June 30 the task being prescribed-area distance flight within an area bounded by turn points at Marfa, Van Horn, Pecos and McCamey. At the close of the day, Allemann had gained on Wally by flying a greater distance within this area and was now sixteen points ahead of him.

Allemann did not hold the lead for long, however. On the sixth contest day, Wally regained first place and left Rudy Allemann sixty-two points in his dust. On the third leg home, flying between 95 and 100 mph and 45 miles out, Wally hit a violent gust that tossed maps and small stones from the floor up around the top of the canopy, while at the same time slamming his landing gear down. Had he lost a wing? Wally considered the parachute he was wearing, but, just as quickly as it had come on, the violent gust passed, and he found that nothing was wrong. He retracted the landing gear, straightened up the mess in the cockpit and finished strong for the day.

On the seventh day, it was George Moffat who suddenly took over the lead. Steadily varying between second and third place over the previous days, Moffat had pushed his scoring point total way up and over Wally's.

The final contest day was a closed-course race from Marfa to McCamey to Van Horn and back to Marfa totaling 344 miles. Moffat again won this contest day with the fastest race-time completion and moved into final standing as the U.S. National Champion. Wally did nearly as well, his speed being second best, and he preserved his second place final standing in the contest. The two contestants who had dominated the contest had come through under immense pressure to prove that they were the best. For Rudy Allemann, however, the day's speed performance was a disappointment that pushed him back to fourth place overall.

The 36th U.S. National Soaring Championships awards banquet was held in the Beta Sigma Phi Building. The Larissa Stroukoff Memorial Trophy, honoring the best goal-and-return flight of the contest, went to Wally Scott, who was also celebrating his birthday. Wally also received a SSA medallion for his second place finish. George B. Moffat Jr. received the Richard C. Dupont Trophy to a standing ovation, celebrating the man who had won the championship against the most formidable pilot competition ever assembled in the United States.

The ASW-12, and its sister ships, would go on to secure a place in sailplane history as one of the highest performance, production fiberglass sailplanes produced during this period of time. Wally would eventually purchase an ASW-12. Ultimately, the ASW-12's lack of dive brakes or spoilers for glide path control and the lack of an integrated water ballast system for enhancing high-speed glide performance would limit its acceptance by pilots, and relegate the ASW-12 to being a museum showpiece.

Showdown Over Gila Bend

Adapted from: Douglas Lamont's adaptation of Wallace Scott's account of his world record 605-mile goal distance flight. Soaring Magazine, January 1970

"I don't like flies, I never have. This one got in while my canopy was still open. I was strapped in and ready to roll, when my final check showed I had no power to my radio or electric variometer. While my son, Wally Jr., was replacing a fuse, I saw the fly near the nose under the fixed section of the canopy. I was busy; I figured I'd get him out later, but the new fuse blew too, and I forgot about him.

"Wally Jr. said, 'Go anyway, Dad. It won't be the first time you've flown cross-country without radio and electric variometer.' It was 11:30 a.m. on August 22, 1969, and I was losing time. I shut the canopy and took off with the fly. On tow, something irritated me. It wasn't the fly, which had come out of hiding and was now buzzing amiably around the cockpit. It wasn't the slow climb – I had ordered that to have time to get a feel for the air. No, something deeper was bothering me, something that might be called, well… *dispossession.*

'When a person fences off a section of the range in this part of the world, no one expects him to give it up without a fuss—even if the claim-jumper is a Texas neighbor. In the Paris archives of the Federation Aeronautique Internationale, my name had been firmly wedded, for half a decade, to the world distance goal flight record for motorless aircraft.

Understandably, I had developed a propriety feeling toward this particular niche of aviation's highest Pantheon, and I wasn't about to hand it over to someone else without a scrap.

'After I reached my release altitude of 3900 feet MSL, a dry thermal over an open rock pit carried me high enough to hop eastward to a newborn cumulus. Having established my point of departure east of the field, I recrossed the airport at about starting-gate altitude and began my flight west. For the next hour, the sleek ASW-12 whisked me over the arid Texas countryside at inter-thermal speeds of 100 mph. The clouds looked better to the right, but that direction was out due to a cold front. I was counting on two low-pressure areas that lay further west over Yuma and Mexico to pull the ground flow around until it was squarely behind me.

"I caught the glint of the Pecos River snaking from north to south across my path. On the other side of the valley, razor-sharp canyons slashed into slopes rising toward the Guadalupe Range. This lay dead ahead and athwart in my course. These mutilated inclines clutched lecherously at the unmarred whiteness of the 12's sinking keel until only 100 feet of altitude remained. With the mountain barrier looming ever higher, the fly became increasingly agitated, darting left to right or to the nose, where he surveyed the danger ahead.

"Several times I tried to scoop him out the canopy's sliding window, but he always evaded me. I got the feeling that he was trying to get somewhere important, so I stopped chasing him. My cockpit friend was a brilliant iridescent green, so I decided to call him 'Greenie.' After a while, he sensed my change of attitude and decided it was safe to climb on the camera shelf near my head. I guess he figured that was the best seat in the house.

"It didn't take me long to find lift and soon we were looking down on the 8,751-foot Guadalupe Peak, Texas' highest mountain. With this first barrier surmounted, Greenie stood quietly on his perch, staring intently ahead as if the sight triggered some dim recollection. I, too, was moved by the beauty of what I saw. I could sense the curvature of the earth. The sky was filled with islands of floating white cumulus. Their dark bases and even spacing formed an arch that bent over the sharp edge of the far horizon. It was like flying in some immense glass bowl where the clouds were painted on the curvature above.

"For me, this was soaring at its best. It was the kind of dependable weather a guy could really count on. On the other side of the Guadalupe, I went bombing along toward El Paso without thinking about the terrain or the absence of civilization below. My mind was on more important matters. Call it a matter of Texas hospitality, but when a visiting tenderfoot from the East by the name of Ben Greene had flown a goal record of 456 miles out of Odessa, Al Parker waited only twenty days until he one-upped him with a new record of 487 miles in his Sisu. Along with certain other things, this breach of Western etiquette held out for a year until I put things straight by taking the record for myself with a 520-mile goal flight in a Ka-6. Well, that was all in the past. I'd lost my record and right now getting it back was the first order of business. I shoved the stick forward a little more.

"The Mexican border finally pinched off Texas at El Paso, and I was now flying over New Mexico. Before I allowed myself to get close enough to feel the inviting moisture of the bases of the clouds, I dropped the nose and shot out into the sunlight again. A man with a score to settle has no time for dalliance.

"I noticed the sky taking on a different texture, and visibility was dropping. Blow-off from thunderstorms? I thought to myself. Through the haze ahead, the sun's backlighting silvered the billowing crests of a towering cloud wall that hid the Chiracahua Range in ominous gloom below. Clouds and mountains straddled my course in common cause against my progress. Greenie's wings quivered nervously, but I bored on, racing to flank the barrier before the clouds cycled and dumped their torrents.

"Which way to turn? Uncertain, I headed directly for the north end of the Chiracahuas, hoping to fly around the storm area, where cloud bases left little clearance above the mountains. In my race to beat the cloud cycle, I burned up my altitude until I sank far below the bases and could see the sunlit ground on the other side toward Tucson. No shadows! That meant no working cu's once I got through. I could be shot down in a blue hole of stable air. I turned my gaze south. There! Yes, on the other side I spotted the comforting silhouettes of cu's moving west, a bridge toward my goal— if I could reach it. I swung southwest, having already crossed into Arizona. Fortunately there was lift, and I attempted to accumulate the 11,000 feet it would take to get me through to the sunny flatlands and the clouds on the other side. This was it!

"Tightening belt and harness, I edged my airspeed dial toward its rough-air redline mark and started for the ridge. The deep cloud build-up above me darkened the cockpit. The ridges suddenly rose sickeningly. I was sinking, or plummeting was more like it. The next half-minute would decide. I watched the growing crests with helpless fascination, as if I were a passenger rather than the master of his craft. A final blurred glimpse of scraggly roots protruding from a fissure in the crest's rocky precipice told me that I must have crossed the summit with 300 feet to spare, too close for comfort.

"For some reason, I looked for Greenie at this moment. I found him sitting on the shelf, hunkered down and unmoving. At first I thought he was immobile from the cold or altitude, but maybe he was scared stiff. I was now far south of the course line and still had nearly 200 miles to cover before I would reach Gila Bend, my declared goal. In my gamble to reach the bridge of cu's, I had left the safety of the main roads and was little more than thirty miles from the Mexican border to the south. Greenie hopped down and ambled along the edge of the map. He didn't look well at all. I picked him up carefully and set him back on the camera shelf, and he just stayed there.

"As we got to a lower level in search of cu's, the cockpit started warming up and the little insect became active again, kicking out his hind legs and preparing his wings. The weather and clouds remained steady now and there were good clouds toward Gila Bend. A tingle went up my spine. The Big One—the world distance record—was there for the taking. Did I want it? What would folks in Odessa say? Greenie leapt off the shelf and flew forward, where he battered desperately against the front of the canopy.

"I thought about abandoning the goal and going for free distance. But, no, I didn't want to say I abandoned it from seventy, thirty or ten miles out. No, if I elected to overfly my goal and get the distance record, I wanted to do it *from directly above the goal.* I sent the ASW-12 hissing under the clouds until the slanting light of the sun was reflected in a silvery, fragmented 'V' by the river at Gila Bend. I had made my goal! On to California. Many times I had envisioned the way the sky would look beyond Gila Bend—now the truth was even better than the dream. I sat back and let my beautiful bird carry me westward. As the minutes ticked on, I had second thoughts. There was little more than an hour of sunlight. I didn't want to fly after dark, so the best I could hope for was 700 miles or a little more. Still enough to break the free-distance record of 647 miles, and I had become attached to breaking those records.

"Finally, knowing full well that I would be criticized by many, I turned my back on the beautiful western sky, delayed my dreams of California for another day and 'from beyond the 1,000 km arc from Odessa,' I returned to Gila Bend, landing with the personal satisfaction of knowing that I had exceeded the world's distance record mileage in point-to-point-and-return soaring flight.

"At four a.m. the next morning, I was sitting in the cockpit of the ASW-12 staying up with the ship waiting for a storm with 50-mph winds to finally abate. A faint buzzing noise from the bottom of the instrument panel intruded on my consciousness. As I leaned forward to get a closer look, Greenie whizzed by like an F-104 vectored for intercept. I grabbed wildly at the empty air. For the briefest moment, I glimpsed an angry black dot disappearing or vanishing into the coppery sky. I recognized the heading—270 degrees west—toward California.

Wally with his son and crew Wally Jr. next to ASW-12 discussing
weather before take-off, Marfa, TX (Photograph by Allen Dutton,
courtesy Boots Scott)

Over Odessa, TX in a Ka 6 E, the glider he flew his 552 mile flight
from Odessa, TX to Casa Grande, AZ in on August 23, 1967

July 26, 1970 ready for take-off in ASW-12 for record flight with Ben Greene

Putting away ASW-12, Marfa, TX 1970
Photograph courtesy National Soaring Museum

1972 Permian High School put MOJO on Wally's glider before his first Smirnoff Derby. He flew the rest of his life as MOJO.

Over Odessa, TX in ASW-20

At Washington, DC banquet in honor of Wally & Ben's 1970 record flight. Left to right: Ben Greene, Werner von Braun, Neil Armstrong, Dr. Ernest Steinoff, Wallace Scott

Over Odessa, TX in ASW-12

1983 family picture: left to right
   Back row: Deby Garner, Seree Whitlow, Dema Moore, Boots & Wally
   Next row: James Garner, Gary Whitlow, Cody Allee (Seree's son),
   Next row: Jamie Garner (Deby's daughter), Jennifer Withlow
   (Seree's daughter), Heile Allee (Seree's daughter),
   Bottom row: Jody Moore (Dema's son), Julibeth Moore (Dema's
   Daughter), Jackson Garner (Deby's son)

Landing ASW-20 at Laredo, TX

July 18, 1979, outlanding in a field 1 mile south of St. John, KS
during Standard Class Nationals

1979 Wally's Schweizer 1-35 (top) on display at Smithsonian Air and
Space Museum in Washighton, DC. It would stay there for 3 years.
Below the 1-35 is Al Parker's Sisu

A ramp kiss. Hutchinson, KS 1979

WALLACE A. SCOTT

1972 promotional shot for 1st Smirnoff Derby. He won 1st place

1998 in ASW-20, taken before his last flight

The World Comes to Marfa

Wally completed a 605.23-mile flight on his trek to Gila Bend, winning back his claim to the 1969 Barringer Award and setting new National and World free distance records. The Larissa Stroukoff Award would also be given to Wally this year. Always in pursuit of making it 1,000 miles straight-out distance in his glider, the biggest challenge was finding an air mass of 1,000 miles around Odessa with conditions that could keep him going all the way to California. On this flight to Gila Bend, he would stay south around the Mexican border to help him gain miles before heading north. On other distance flights, he would use an artificial horizon (instrument used in an aircraft to inform the pilot of the orientation of the aircraft relative to the earth) to allow him to fly into a cloud using the additional height in the clouds to help him gain distance.

An artificial horizon is an instrument using a gyroscope, but Wally's "artificial horizon" was just a piece of tape on the top of the cockpit instrument panel that was lined up with the horizon before take-off. In controlled airspace, gliders are prohibited from flying in clouds due to the dangers of disorientation and chance of hitting another aircraft. But Wally was not about to let that keep him from his 1,000-mile flight. Luckily in the days when most of the air space between Texas and California was uncontrolled and free from other aircraft, the areas when he would have to declare his whereabouts to air traffic controllers on the radio were few and far between. Eventually, accepting the rules of physics, Wally would break down and purchase a true artificial horizon and installed it in his instrument panel. Wally would continue to make attempt after attempt, using all the tricks in his bag to get to that 1,000-mile flight. Another busy summer flying season slowed in the fall, and Wally returned his focus to his home life.

Wally Jr., who continued to spend every free moment crewing for and flying alongside his dad, was now nineteen years old, graduated from high school, and attending Odessa Community College. He would later graduate with honors from Texas Tech University in Lubbock, TX. Seree had graduated from high school in 1966 and was now attending Texas Christian University in Fort Worth, Texas. The artist of the family, she had her paintings put in permanent archives at TCU. Later in the year, she would marry John Allee. Dema and Deby graduated high school in May of 1969. Deby married James Garner right away and went to Houston, Texas, to attend Rice University. But, after a serious rape incident involving another college freshman, she would decide to hold off on school, and she became a Dictaphone typist at an insurance company. Dema went to Baylor University and, upon graduation from Baylor, she would marry Joe Moore. She returned to school to get her masters in Education. With only Wally Jr. still at home, the house felt empty to Wally and Boots, but they kept their MOJO tradition and were busy working at the family-owned theatres and flying.

For years, American soaring pilots had been bidding for the next World Championships to take place on American soil, an event that had never occurred before. After waiting patiently, in 1970 it was finally decided that the 12th World Soaring Championships would be held in Marfa, Texas. This was the perfect opportunity for the Americans to combine strength and maintain their place at the top of international soaring, on their turf and on their terms.

The individuals competing on the U.S. Team for the 12th World Championships were under the leadership of seven-time U.S. National Soaring Champion Dick Johnson, and consisted of George B. Moffat Jr., Wally Scott, A.J. Smith, and Rudy Allemann. The pilots, all of whom had become close personal friends of Wally's, were not here for the laid-back camaraderie found at other competitions. Together, they represented the U.S. Team, but individually they represented the best in the country competing to be the best in the world. With a second place finish in the 1964 and 1969 Nationals, his sixth-place finish at the World Championships in England and two world goal marks, first in his Ka-6 and most recently in the ASW-12, Wally had more than earned his second seeding on the team.

George Moffat, the number one seeded pilot, was without a doubt the best competition pilot in the country. Moffat was known for his generally reserved demeanor; his biggest competitor, Wally, was just the opposite. Wally was known to the soaring community as one of the friendliest among them, but a focused competitor to be reckoned with. A.J. Smith, the defending World Champion and third seeded on the team, was distinctive for his charming after-dinner speeches and his 'hard-and-hungry' intense contest manner. A.J., like Wally, had competed on the 1965 U.S. Team. Lastly, Rudy Allemann was the new boy on the team. At 38, Allemann was the only member not to have competed on a U.S. Team before, but he was known for holding his own alongside Moffat and Wally during the Marfa Nationals in 1969.

With twenty-six countries and eight-two sailplanes represented, the 12th World Championships started off with a bit of a loss because the Peruvian team had to leave due to a massive earthquake back home. As the remaining countries gathered their teams and sailplanes, the sailplanes once again became the highlight of the contest on the ground. Aircraft, with names sounding as foreign as the countries they represented, included the Libelle from the German company Glasflügel, the Urupemas from Brazil and the Sisu from the U.S. One of the main attractions was a new Kestrel, a 22-meter (wingspan of 72 feet) ship flown by German pilot Walter Neubert.

Wally, flying his own recently purchased ASW-12, had a worse than expected first contest day, but not quite as disappointing as George Moffat's. Wally, finishing 17th, and Moffat 21st. Both knew they had botched the first day, which could be nearly impossible to recover from. Surprisingly, at the end of Day 1 it was the Poles in the lead! They had slipped out of the top in the past championships, but here they were winning the top spots in both the Open and Standard class.

On the morning of the second contest day, the third place finisher of Day 1, Neubert, still had not reported back. He had landed out on a farm somewhere and, though he was armed with a card provided to all contestants that did not speak English, he found it quite useless because the farmhouse on the land turned out to be empty. The card read, 'This man is a glider pilot taking part in the 12th World Soaring Championships... If he is not proficient in speaking English, he may need your assistance.... in contacting his crew. Any assistance you can give him will be greatly appreciated and offer you the opportunity to demonstrate American hospitality on a person-to-person basis to our visitors.' Had the family been home this card might have worked, but as no one was there, and Neubert was too afraid to enter the farmhouse on his own (due to countless Texan cowboy movies) he slept in his glider.

After getting help the next morning, Neubert arrived at 3:08 p.m., more than two hours after the last of the open class gliders had launched. As nine people worked to repair the glider, which had taken a beating on his farm landing, Neubert strapped on a parachute, wolfed down a sandwich, and was on the runway for take-off 31½ minutes later. The valiant efforts of Neubert and crew, however, could not prevail against the weather and, unable to connect, the Kestrel was soon on the ground again.

Wally Scott was the first open-class finisher of the second day at thirty-seven minutes after four p.m., with Moffat right on his tail. The task was an out-and-return speed run north to Pecos and back. Wally and Moffat, who were team-flying, had been in contact via radio. But, Wally had slipped in quite a few minutes before his team mate and competitor. Both pilots moved into the top ten. The recovery in standings had begun. Team flying, practiced anywhere except in SSA sanctioned contest, was allowed during the World Championships, as these are flown under the international rules of the FAI (Federation Aeronautic Internationale). Pilots flying as a team are allowed to share information and support one another throughout the race. The desired result is to have pilots perform as a team, fly their best, and help the team to win. Each country is assigned its own radio frequency but because all frequencies can be listened to by all teams, the challenge is coming up with codes for the communications so competitors can't understand what the team members are saying to each other. Each morning, a separate US team meeting was held to discuss the code words for the day.

On the third contest day, wet weather made it difficult for everyone, in general, and for Wally, in particular. He continued to make attempts in the rain, mostly to support Moffat who needed his help confronting the weather. Wally took off for his final attempt at 5:45 p.m., after A.J., Allemann, and Moffat had all finished the day's task. An hour later, he landed back at the field, unable to get away. His trouble this day placed him in 30th overall, while Moffat's first place finish took him to sixth place. Wally accepted his third day defeat and knew he would have no chance at finishing first. At this point, he would aim to finish in the top ten—"the winners circle."

Moffat was running a fever on the fourth day of competition, but that did not deter him from giving his most remarkable performance, yet upping his average speed to 66.2 mph and winning the day. This performance gained him a third place in the overall standing. Not one to be overshadowed by much, Wally finished second for the day and completed the course twice, when only once was necessary.

The fifth day posed some problems for Wally, including a ten-mile detour that cost Wally at least ten minutes overall. Over Valentine, Texas, Moffat and Wally teamed up, flying seven to ten miles apart and carefully navigating their way through rainstorms. Moffat finished the day in first, yet again, with Wally close behind at a remarkable second place for the day! The U.S. Team finished first, second, third and fifth for the day, their most exciting achievement, so far. After a rest day competition continued with the sixth contest day. With a day full of thunderstorms, Moffat and Scott dropped to overall fifth and sixth respectively.

On the seventh day, it was decided the task would be a declared out-and-return speed task to Pecos and back. The pilots were all worried about the weak thermals and low cloud base. Proving not to be much of a challenge for Wally, he finished third for the day and pulled himself up to a 13th place standing overall. Moffat, playing it safe in the weather, found himself in eighth place for the day.

The task choice for the eighth day could not have been better for Wally. The Task Committee sent the contestants east on a triangular speed task and return in the direction of Odessa, with Sierra Blanca and Fort Stockton as turn points. The weather looked promising, and the pilots were enthusiastic about the task. Wally and Moffat waited around for the cloud base to get higher, and then Wally started out first. Around Mt. Livermore, where the best thermals of the day had been expected, Wally was surprised to find the worst thermals of the day. Wally and Moffat, team flying, would make a thirty-five-mile final glide to the finish line.

Moffat decided to play it safe and deviated north to Fort Davis. Wally took the straight line, got pretty low but found a strong thermal to beat Moffat to the finish by a few minutes. Moffat's higher average speed, however, earned him 1,000 points for the day, and he beat all the day's competitors. Wally finished third for the day.

A speed task was once again assigned for the ninth and final contest day. Wally and Moffat talked about the upcoming flight and started within minutes of each other staying close throughout the flight. Over the mountains of Lobo, Texas, Wally split off going south and Moffat continued straight. But, after this short break, they met up again. Moffat was high on final and, in fear of overshooting the runway, he had to use his tail drag parachute. The parachute didn't open, however, and Moffat barely was able to stop before he ran out of runway. He came in first place again, with Wally placing second. In the end, Moffat became the new World Champion, and Wally worked his way up from 13th to accomplish his goal with a winner's-circle, ninth-place finish.

For both Wally and Walter Neubert, one bad day was the difference between first place and barely making the top ten. Always a non-conformist, the constraints of competition flying, like those at the Marfa World

Championships, kept Wally more committed to free distance flying. The milder rules and restrictions of free distance gave Wally the flexibility to alter his flying to the varying weather demands and also allowed him the opportunity to fly wherever he pleased once he was in the air. When the competition season came to a close, Wally was eager to return to his first priority—breaking distance records.

The next distance challenge would be the most important and memorable of his life. A fellow glider pilot and longtime friend, Ben Greene expressed to Wally the desire to set a distance record. Wally proposed a dual simultaneous distance flight that, if successful, would land both of their names on the Barringer. Sherman Griffith says of this particular flight, 'Everyone remembers where they were when Kennedy was shot, or 9/11. I remember where I was when Wally and Ben completed this flight.'

Double Record

Adapted from: Wallace Scott and Ben Greene, "The Big One" Soaring Magazine, February 1971

"Ben and I had been looking for the day when we could go record hunting together. Our plans were to declare a goal far enough out to win both distance and goal distance records at the same time. If we got separated, we agreed the first one to reach the goal should have the choice of either landing or going on for more distance—leaving the goal record to the other.

"Our ships were in a constant state of preparedness. On the night of July 25th, I called the weatherman on duty at the Midland-Odessa terminal. He said the next day looked promising. Ben was more excited than usual when he called, but he was worried about the cold front moving into Nebraska—it could cut us off and shut the door north. We decided to meet at the airport.

"When Ben drove up, I was already securing my barograph, maps, and duffle in the ASW-12. He was still slightly worried about the front cutting us off. Ben was for declaring Broken Bow, Nebraska, but I wanted Thedford because it was across the 700-mile line. We flipped a coin; it came out Thedford, so we both declared it for our goal. Ben insisted I take the first tow.

"Just after take-off, I realized I hadn't turned on my barograph so I made a quick abort and landed without using the drag chute. Wally Jr.

159

caught on fast and got on channel 122.8 MHz to declare an emergency, so that the endless stream of traffic would wait for us. All this took but a few minutes, but a feeling of guilt came over me when I saw Ben standing there watching the skies blossom with beautiful cu's.

"After the second tow, I immediately started cruising north at high speed. Ben came over the radio on tow and said to the tow pilot Wally Jr., 'Take me to the same place your dad released.' Ben was only a few minutes behind. Conditions were good from the start; we were being helped along by a brisk wind. There were widely spaced cu's, but no streeting, yet. Pretty soon, Ben called me.

'How's it going buddy, and where are you?' I relayed my position.

'Have you taken a look at our ground speeds?' I knew we were over seventy miles out and had not yet been gone an hour, so I answered, 'Pretty good, I reckon, but they should get better.' About 200 miles out, the cloud bases rose, and some streeting started. The only trouble was the cloud streets ran slightly west of our course-line heading. I followed them nevertheless. Ben came on the radio again, 'Where are you now?' he said. I told him. 'You're flying pretty far left of course.'

"Ben had drawn a line to our goal, and I had failed to do so. I asked him where the course line lay in reference to Amarillo, which was about seventy-five miles south of the Oklahoma border.

"'It is practically over Amarillo,' he said. I was above Dimmitt, nearly twenty-five miles west of the flight line. I radioed Ben, 'Okay, I'll get back on course.' There was a rather wide hole of clear air east of the cloud street where I was cruising, but I had plenty of altitude, so I crossed without trouble. By the time I reached the little town of Canyon, twenty miles south of Amarillo, the lift was still higher. It was Sunday. We had radio conversations with glider pilots flying locally around the panhandle area. They wished us luck. We were making good time and passed Amarillo a little after 1:00 p.m. We could make twenty- and thirty-minute glides at high speed and then get back the altitude lost with just a few turns in the strong lift. Cloudbases were never much above 10,000 or 10,500 MSL all day.

"I started having trouble with my radio. To save the battery, I decided to turn it off and check with Ben every fifteen minutes. The good clouds and streets lasted across Oklahoma, but ended about sixty miles after we crossed the border into Kansas. We started using individual clouds that still looked fairly decent, but the lift was getting weaker. At one point in the northern part of the state, I had to make a long glide to reach what appeared to be a promising cumulus. The cloud looked as if it was beginning to evaporate, and I began to worry. My misgivings were short lived however, and over Hoxie, I centered a 700-fpm lift that stayed good right up to base.

"The front and its associated clouds had grown until their anvils and easterly blow-off had hidden the ground below. These shadows were obscuring whatever clouds were beneath. I wanted a first-hand look before abandoning our goal. When Ben called, I said, 'Say Buddy, that front looks as if it is about over McCook (just across the Nebraska border). We might consider heading more to the east. I'll go a little further to see how bad the front looks and then decide. Will call you in a few minutes.'

"The closer I got, the worse it looked. I was out in the wide void preceding the front and began to worry that I might have worked myself into a trap. I was saved by a weak, dry thermal that put me back up to 9,500 feet. I called Ben, 'Well, buddy, it don't look too good. I'm heading east to try for the clouds on our right.'

"Ben wanted me to make my own choice. He said, 'Don't let me talk you into anything. You might be able to make our goal, but North Platte is on our course line, and I just called flight service there. They reported thunderstorms in all quadrants with lightning cloud-to-ground – the only thing left out was cloud-to-glider. I told him his change of heading to the northeast was the right decision, 'We may not be able to go as far as we would like,' I said. Ben fired right back, 'We ain't through, yet.'

"We had been separated by many miles, but when Ben told me he was heading toward a good-looking cloud at Hastings, I was close enough to see it. From my vantage point in the west, I could tell the clouds were decaying and motionless. Ben's cloud was the only active one around, and it was a beauty. I relayed that I was working toward the same cloud. Ben figured I was throwing miles away and radioed, 'No, no! Don't come back. Keep going!' But, it was a necessity. It was the only good one around.

"It was a race toward the cu and the sunlight. Suddenly, there was an unmistakably flash of sunlight on white wings and for the first time in eight hours and 600 miles, we were in visual contact. Moments later we were circling together in the lift the cloud had promised. Ben got out his charts and saw that we were crossing the penciled red line he had marked for World Record Distance.

"Anyone on 123.3 MHz at that time might have been concerned by the 'Yahoos' and 'whoo-ees' and giggles coming from the two adults, but this was an unusual occasion. I offered to throw some food over to Ben who had eaten the last of his space sticks hours before. Ben quipped back that he wished he could pitch over his bank-and-turn instrument to me. I had forgotten all about his gyro. We were still under the cloud. If he climbed into the cloud, he could reach perhaps 20,000 feet, and I would have to stay below base because I did not have any blind-flying, gyro instrument. I apologized and told him to take the next thermal on up. Ben replied "We will stay together." We decided to try to make it to Columbus where an old pal, pilot Frank Lilly, was on the ground waiting. After identifying us from the radio, he told us to make it to Columbus where there was promised hangar space out of the weather. Ben and I were a long way out, and we worried about making it in a flat glide. We went to flap position three for best glide performance, and I began to relax as I looked down and watched the ground fairly scooting by. Bless those tailwinds.

"We got to the airport with 2,000 feet. We could have gone on for maybe another twenty miles, but we risked the rain and lightning belt that was following us closely. Our crews were at least half a day behind, so we decided to land at Columbus. Then it occurred to us that if we didn't both land at exactly the same time, the one who touched down first would hold the record and the other would have to fly ten more kilometers to beat him (by the FAI rules).

"I told Ben, 'Great, we'll make a no-chute landing.[3] Come in long, Ben, I'll trail behind. Let me know when you are ready to touch down.' Then we flared out on the air cushion above the runway. I waited until I heard Ben key his mike, then I dobbed the '12 on the asphalt. He said, 'I'm on,' and I said, 'Me too.' After nine plus hours in the air, I lifted myself out of cockpit and onto the ground. A sign near us read, 'Welcome to Columbus, Nebraska,' and, as I looked up, I saw Ben running toward me with a smile on his face.

---

[3] Note: The ASW-12 was the only production sailplane to employ only a drag chute for glide path control. It did not have spoilers or dive brakes.

Wallace Scott and Ben Greene in front of a map showing
their 716.95 mile record flight from Odessa, TX
to Columbus, NE on July 26, 1970

From Sea to Shining Sea

With the help of each other, Wally and Ben reached their goal and set a new National and World Distance Record with 716.95 miles. The Barringer Trophy for 1970 would read Benjamin W. Greene and Wallace A. Scott. This would be the first time the trophy would be shared by a team of pilots. Their record held until 1977 when Wally tied it. And, the record was finally broken in 1984 by Michael S. Koerner. Also in 1970, Wally received his first Exceptional Achievement Award from the Soaring Society of America and set a new World Goal-and-Return record on a flight from Odessa to Pampa and return at 534 miles.

Wally won the Barringer again the next year on September 11, 1971, on a flight from Odessa to Estrella, Arizona, at 578.48 miles cross-country. The following year, however, it would be another Wally Scott that would steal the Barringer. Wally Jr., who was now twenty-two years old and had been following in his father's footsteps for years, had finally beaten him at his own game. Wally Jr. won the 1972 Barringer with a distance flight of 634.85 miles. All in the family, Wally Sr. would take the Barringer back in 1973 and again in 1975 with a 600.9-mile flight to Imperial, Nebraska.

The Barringer had become more than a love affair for the Scott family. It had become a long-standing relationship. The affair would persist, but a new challenge was about to present itself. The first-ever, transcontinental Smirnoff Sailplane Derby was introduced in 1972. Being a race from California to Maryland that was to be flown in separate daily legs while given less than a month's time to complete, this was unlike anything Wally had ever done before. The derby was the brainchild of Ben Dunn at Heublein, Inc., makers of Smirnoff vodka. Smirnoff found that it was relatively inexpensive to sponsor a needy sport, and it generated significant positive PR and advertisement. Dunn got in contact with Ed Butts, a retired Air Force Major who had conducted many soaring meets, and Paul Bikle, the former head of the NASA Flight Research Center at Edwards Air Force Base also an avid soaring enthusiast.

As captain of the U.S. soaring team, Bikle was looking for money to finance the U.S. team for the next world championships in Yugoslavia. Butts agreed to recruit some of the top soaring pilots, and Smirnoff agreed to give the U.S. team $6,000 and each pilot that competed $2,000 for personal and crew expenses. The deal was made, and the race was on. Now all they had to do was find some pilots.

They didn't get all the top pilots, but they got most of them. Wally Scott, of course, was a likely candidate and was lately being referred to as 'the MOJO man.' With two National Championships under his belt and a current world distance record, Wally was one of the many soaring buffs present as the contestants assembled in California on May 1, 1972. Among other pilots that were competing was Bikle himself, known for his world altitude record of 42,267 feet and for saying, "I could have gone higher, but it got kind of cold up there," (It was 65 degrees below zero). A.J. Smith, known as much for his obedience and dedication to the sport as his world championship win, was among them as well. Then there was John Ryan and his signature pink golf hat that 'won' him the 1962 national championship. His daughter had given him the hat, and since the win, he had never flown without it. Besides the heavy-weight pilots in the race, the sailplanes were, as usual, the next huge attraction.

John Ryan's German Nimbus 2 was the highest performance aircraft at the race, and behind that, Wally's ASW-12, a Glasflügel Kestrel and a Swiss Diamant 18 claimed performances that were about even. A.J. Smith was flying with a passenger in a high-performance, two-place, fiberglass sailplane manufactured by Caproni of Italy, and Bikle was flying a home-built, all-metal adaptation of a Schreder HP-14 that had about a 15% performance handicap. Bikle's advantage, however, was his knowledge of east coast flying and the Allegheny Mountains. The Allegheny Mountains, spanning the entire east coast, very nearly stopped the U.S. Air Mail before it even began, and now Wally and the others would be flying through the same area known as 'The Graveyard' to pilots. The only difference was they would be doing it without an engine.

The race began in Los Angeles under the baking sun right around noon. Wally and his crew, Boots, Wally Jr. and Dema spoke in what they called 'MOJO code,' which was code for 'Wally's gonna do so well, we won't have to worry about retrieving him from an out-landing.' Competitor teams on the Derby used codes to hide their pilots' progress. Wally's crew believed their pilot could do anything and didn't need secret code language. This multi-leg trek across the country would be taxing on not only the sailplane pilots, but the crews as well. Following the sailplane's flight track as closely as possible, they would be close by in case they needed to retrieve a glider after an off-airport, out-landing. The extreme variance in flying from one end of the country to the other meant the crew had to adjust the glider for every climate. In California, they discovered spraying a little wax on the leading edge of the wing kept bugs and dirt from sticking to the wing. The dead bugs caused drag and slowed down the sailplane. Before the Smirnoff began, a woman that was involved at NASA saw Boots spraying regular Pledge onto the front of the wings of the sailplane and informed Boots that at NASA they did the exact same thing for the space shuttle. They were never without a bottle of Pledge in the crew car again.

On the first leg to Phoenix, the home of John Ryan, Ryan beat Wally in by an hour. A.J., Bikle and others didn't make it. A.J., who had a knack for turning a bad situation into a good one, said, 'I looked for the bluest pool and the biggest bar.' He landed at Los Caballeros, a resort on Vulture Mine Road west of Wickenburg.

On the next leg to Las Cruces, New Mexico, it was Ryan once again who beat Wally to the finish by ten seconds. The next day, however, it was Wally's turn to race home. He won the leg into Odessa and never lost a race leg after that. After a still, no lift day that left the gliders on the ground, Butts decided to take the race by road to Dallas where it rained for three days before they headed by road to Tulsa. The schedule demanded timely appearances at key metropolitan locations, so if the weather was bad, the teams progressed by car with the gliders being towed in their trailers behind the team automobiles.

From Tulsa, the hope was to make it to St. Louis, but unpredictable flying conditions made it doubtful whether anyone could even make it sixty-five miles. Gliders landed out as short as fifty miles outside of Tulsa, but Wally made it ninety-five miles, which meant 1,000 points for the leg and a commanding lead. Each leg was scored as a separate race. He again took wins on the legs into Joliet, Illinois, and Bryan, Ohio. For the next leg of the race, the Smirnoff took a detour off course to add another leg onto the trip, but more importantly, to accept a party invitation from Bob Fergus who was another soaring enthusiast. The flight was a quick one, and the party was worth the additional leg. The next day, the crowd again found themselves immersed in rain, so the caravan trailered to Akron-Canton, Ohio. After three days of waiting out the weather, Butts put it to the pilots –skip the next leg and go for the last leg tomorrow? After some hesitation the answer came back yes. With enough bad luck on Wally Scott's side and enough good luck on theirs, someone might be able to overtake Wally's 680-point lead.

On Thursday May 18, a day behind the original Smirnoff schedule, the sailplanes took off with weather conditions looking murky. A heavy ground fog in Pittsburgh left the pilots with only one option, which was to fly over the mountains and eyeball the conditions for improvement the entire time. As expected, most of the pilots didn't make it beyond the lower slope. But, Bikle worked the lift to power his way up from fifth to second place. After a close call over Latrobe, where the crew thought he was about to land, it was Wally Scott who defied the weather flying through lightning and a thunderstorms to come out the champion. It must have been the MOJO. After a scary day for his crew, Boots Scott flew into the arms of her champion once he was safely on the ground. The winner of the first-ever

Smirnoff Sailplane Derby, Wally Scott had a whole new passion to develop. He would continue to fly the Smirnoff, placing second the next year, but would be unable to attend the following year.

PART 3 – THE THIRD LEG: 1974 - 2003

Matters of the Heart

The 3rd Smirnoff Sailplane Derby would be underway soon and Wally was busy getting in shape for what would be his third trip across the country. Getting ready included being physically in shape for the upcoming days. On Tuesday morning March 12, 1974 at the age of 50, Wally was busy on an exercise machine as Boots was ironing on the porch. He finished up after 30 minutes on the bike and yelled to Boots that he was heading to the store for some Cornish game hens, since his niece, Lodema, would be joining them for dinner.

Wally crossed the living room and proceeded to the bathroom, when he cried out for Boots. When she got to the bathroom she saw Wally, red in the face lying on the ground. Her mind quickly went back to her training as a girl scout leader and to an old first-aid adage, 'If the face is red raise the head, if the face is pale raise the tail,' and she quickly raised his head. She helped Wally get to their bed, and, when she called the doctor, he told her to get him to the emergency room. Boots remembers, 'You know they tell you not to speed when on your way to the emergency room, but all I remember is I drove as fast as I possibly could and Wallace even told me to go faster.' Fast she went on their way to the Odessa Regional Medical Center where the doctor met them at the door. Wally was immediately given a 'hot shot' of morphine, and then he had his heart attack in the hospital.

Always very careful and concerned about his health, except for years of smoking, which he promptly gave up, Wally treated his recovery with great care. He did miss out on the Smirnoff that year and countless other flights that could have been made that summer and the next. But, Wally did as the doctors told him: taking long walks, eating healthy and living a generally low-key lifestyle. Wally would focus on his health and his family for a few years before returning to soaring in the 1976 Smirnoff Derby.

Though most of their kids had moved away, they were all still in Texas and remained close to their parents and visited often. Seree, now in Houston, would soon divorce her first husband John Allee and would marry Gary Whitlow and move to Hawkins, TX. Wally Jr. would graduate with honors from Texas Tech and become a schoolteacher in Midland, Texas for 13 years. He eventually went to work for Texas Instruments for another 20 years. After his marriage in 1977, he placed his soaring pursuits and interests on hold. He eventually moved to Sherman, TX north of Dallas. Dema would remain in Waco teaching art at Midway High School and Deby would eventually make it back to Odessa to live for awhile before ultimately settling close to Dema in Waco and working as a secretary at Midway High School. As the grandchildren began to enter the picture, Wally and Boots made an even stronger effort to be surrounded by family. The crewing responsibility, once again, fell to Boots.

Soon the grandchildren would replace the children and accompany Boots on the road chasing Wally in his glider during the summer. As soon as it was possible, Wally passed his FAA medical and successfully argued his way into getting his pilot's license reinstated. A physical, 10 years later in preparation for a trip to fly the Chilean Andes, would find no sign of his heart attack. He never smoked again, but he did take to dipping snuff. After a full recovery, Wally would be ready just in time to take another stab at his third Smirnoff Sailplane Derby and begin preparations in April of 1976.

Hog the Days

Adapted from: Wallace Scott, "The 1976 Smirnoff Derby"
Soaring Magazine, August 1976

"It all started about D-day minus forty-five. Paul Schweizer called and asked if I would be interested in flying a winner in this year's Smirnoff Sailplane Derby. He wanted to build a 1-35A, a modified version of the 1-35 with a few new ideas off the drawing board, and he needed a pilot to fly it in the derby. Since I did not have a ready-to-go Standard Class Bird, and as there is no other company I would rather see win than Schweizer's, I accepted.

"Boots and I had a good feeling about this year's contest because of a few things such as recuperation from an illness, the road back and all that jazz. The 1-35 would be ready by April 15 of this year, 1976, early enough to give me time to do comparison flying with my ASW-12. By doing this with Wally Jr. at the controls of the '12, I planned to learn 1-35 flying techniques, flap settings for climbing as well as cruising, instrumentation, etc. The '12 had been sold, but delivery was to be after some hoped-for comparison flying. As is nearly always the case, a few snags developed, delaying the delivery of the 1-35 for about a week, and Wally and I took our last flights in the '12 before it left for the West Coast and its new owner. The departure brought quite a tear or two from my family and me.

"On D-day minus thirteen, I took delivery of the 1-35 at Caddo Mills, near Dallas. On April 22, and we left immediately for Odessa with the beautiful green-trimmed 1-35. The next day was unflyable because of the weather, but our steed was in Odessa, and we got acquainted during the next few days. The water ballast system had not been completed at the factory for lack of new inboard and outboard pressure valves. I have never flown with water, so the practice that I needed most was impossible. [4] It would have to wait until I got to El Mirage to receive the valves and install them. My three days of practice in Odessa were with unknown quantities of water and were pretty much useless except for helping me get the feel of the ship.

"On D-day minus four, we left Odessa for California, hoping for two more days of practice, but with water. I have never been so well equipped for a contest. The Schweizer people came through with the rest of instrumentation (to my specifications), plus redundant systems such as spare radio, spare battery, spare this, and spare that. My good friend Red Austin had overhauled my crew radio and had built and installed a new 3-db gain antenna to go along with my trusty old antenna for redundancy. I had a brand new Chevrolet station wagon that had been especially designed with heavy-duty everything. We were equipped with a new Citizens brand radio (and a new fuzz buster radar signal for the smokies.) My crew was to be Boots, and my niece Lodema James. Good wife, good crew, good equipment, good everything. The only unknown at this point was the 1-35 and me. How would we get along?

"We arrived in El Mirage, CA by 14:00 on Saturday, the day of the opening party for Californians and the Smirnoff. First things first, we greeted many old West Coast friends and met a few new ones. Next on the agenda was getting the water ballast valves installed. Ted Schirtzinger, the

---

[4] Note: Many high-performance gliders have the capability of adding water ballast, by carrying water in built-in tanks or water bags in the wings. A glider with water ballast achieves the same glide ratio, but at a higher speed than a glider without water. Higher speeds are dependent on weather conditions and prevalence of thermals, water ballast usually is not used in weak thermals because a heavy glider will not climb as well as a lighter glider.

El Mirage FBO, had been kind enough to fly to L.A. to pick up the valves. But alas, they were the wrong kind with incorrect pressures. At least they fit, but there were no installation instructions. By now, the El Mirage hangar was becoming over-crowded with partygoers, so we retreated to Ann and Gus Briegleb's hangar to escape the hustle and bustle. Gus put everything at my disposal, and the new valves were finally installed. On D-day minus two, we were finally going to fly with water ballast.

"'The written instructions were, "attach garden hose to 1¼ inch plastic hose, open vent valve, and fill.' We filled the left wing with no problems, but the right wing was a different matter. The water came too fast, the vent valve began spewing over everything, Boots started screaming that the wing was leaking, and when I looked up the wing skin looked like a balloon. I hit the dump valve – too late. The damage had been done. I'd popped about 12 rivets and created numerous external water leaks.

"'To heck with it,' I told myself, 'I'll fly anyway.' And I did, for about thirty minutes and then straight into the ground for a landing at Pearblossom south of El Mirage. The other Smirnoff pilots were jabbering about the tremendous lift at 13,000 feet and there I was dumping water on final for an ignominious landing! Lodema James and her husband Bill had helped launch me at El Mirage, and you can imagine how I felt when Bill drove up at Pearblossom. He had driven over for a little glider flying, and needless to say, I immediately swore him to secrecy. Getting back into the air as soon as possible, I once again acknowledged radio calls with the confession that I had turned my radio off for awhile.

"D-day minus one was spent making repairs and filling the wings with water again for another try. The other Smirnoff's had their own problems, and I was the only one to fly this day. I just barely was able to remain aloft with thirty-five gallons of water (a partial load) and gradually worked my way over to the mountains to finally top out near the Cucamonga wilderness. 'WA, this is Smirnoff Ground.' Big Ed Butts, the Derby Competition Director, was calling. 'This is WA, Big Ed, but I'm sorry to say that WA is not my call sign this year. My glider competition number is 62.' Ed, remembering 1972 and 1973, said, 'Okay you will be MOJO.' I landed after a three and a half hour flight, and things were looking up. That evening we drove on to L.A.

"May 4, D-day, dawned with low, low clouds and drizzle. My crew and I, being new to the glider and water game, drove to Whiteman Airpark early and assembled and loaded the 1-35 with water, even though things looked bleak indeed. The morning wore on, and Big Ed finally called us all together for a briefing, which sounded like a distance day. Our first goal was Carefree Airport, north of Phoenix. A few blue holes opened in the overcast to permit take-off, but to get us away from the marine air, the release point had to be Rabbit Dry Lake, some miles east of Pearblossom. Things felt pretty stable. Paul Bikle was having radio problems, so I called for the rendezvous as all six gliders and tow planes formed a half-mile circle.

"It was time for the race to begin. After the countdown to zero, everyone went for the mountains near Big Bear Lake. My plan called for watching the local west coast pilots, but they did what I would have done anyway. The thermals were small, choppy and not good. Leaving the mountains, I headed for the first town in the pass and the safety of the airport and arrived there with 1000 feet. I saw another glider ahead and a little higher. It proved to be Danny Pierson's Nugget AU also in deep trouble, but a little bump was found, some water was released to lighten the glider, and we were saved. Cu's started forming ahead, and soon what had started as a distance day began looking like a speed dash.

"The weather remained this way to Parker, Arizona, where we ran into overdevelopment that slowed us down, and, suddenly, it was a distance day again. Soon my altimeter was unwinding at 1,000 fpm down while the raindrops took their toll. My glide ended atop Moon Mountain, thirty miles south of Parker. I was 3,000 feet above ground, and thought I might just reach the clouds another ten to fifteen miles ahead. If I didn't, I would be in deep trouble. I elected to try and remain aloft over the mountain ridges and await the sunshine, but I gradually sank to below ridge level until landing became inevitable.

"There were plenty of fields just to the west. As I headed for them, I looked down to find a duster strip directly below. I just had time to lower the gear and land! The rancher's name was Jordan. He was a pilot, had a Cessna 182, and professed a yearning to fly gliders. He offered to tow me to Carefree, but I declined. Looking back on the proposition, it might have been fun to have done it and basked in quasi-glory before a final confession. But, I really don't think Big Ed would have approved.

"My crew had the first of several hard days. We de-rigged in the dark, and drove on to Carefree for a 4:30 a.m. check in and an offer of fresh milk and sandwiches. We were famished and tired, but got only five hours of sleep. Nobody had finished. Dan Pierson took first by flying 242 of the course's 342 miles. I was in last place for the day, and my 150 miles were only good for 430 points.

"On the second contest day, Laz Horvath arrived, and I offered to let him fly the 1-35 in exchange for his knowledge of 1-35 flying and flap settings. He agreed, took the ship for a forty-five-minute flight and liked it. I took his advice and won the task. The day's forecast predicted cu's with 7500 MLS bases. With much of the terrain near or above this level, I offered to exchange jobs with director Ed Butts. He declined, saying that I wouldn't like his job. 'Well,' I thought, 'who the hell would enjoy flying over the terrain between Carefree and Globe, Arizona in this weather? It even scared most twin engine pilots at flight level two four zero.' But we did.

"Over the mountains south of Silver City, I became enmeshed in 40-mph westerly winds. It was my turn to climb out of a hole, and I did so slowly. Eventually the wind helped pushed me past Rudy, the frontrunner of the race. I worked anything and everything that came along, but slowly sank to within a few hundred feet of the highway. Glancing down, I saw a safe landing place – an old abandoned inspection station. The off-ramp had been fenced over, but I could see that the west gate had been torn down, so I went in. It was about 55 degrees, and, with a 40-mph wind, the chill factor was much colder. I hid out of the wind in the old abandoned telephone-booth-size office until I figured my crew would be coming. I then went over to stand on the highway and had a two-hour wait for them to show. When they did arrive, they had hot coffee and a sandwich. I'd flown the furthest of the day – 287 miles – and won my first race of the Derby, though I was in third in overall standing.

"A weak start on the third day took me fifteen miles from the start before coming down without catching any lift. Boots and Lodema were there within minutes, and we drove back to the airport for a restart just as the clouds were clearing. My flight was relatively calm, and I was in contact with Nan 6, my crew's radio call sign, the entire way. Unbeknownst to me and much to the amusement of Smirnoff Ground and Paul Bikle, my entire conversation with Nan 6 was being heard by all. They busted in on our conversation saying, 'MOJO, this is Smirnoff Ground. What is going on up there?' 'Good gosh, Ed,' I answered, "Have you been listening to all of this?'

'Yes I have, and it's all down on tape,' Big Ed came back.

'Oh Lordy,' I said.

"Ed advised me that if I ever got back to civilization and wanted to make a highway landing, there was a lot of construction with many obstacles, markers, and equipment that ran for miles. 'Nan 6,' I asked 'How close together are those highway construction markers?' Boots said they looked awfully close together – about forty feet apart. Lodema disagreed, and thought them to be about 100 feet apart. This didn't sound promising for a highway landing, but when I edged on over the highway I could see that they were about 200 yards apart. A highway landing was possible, and would make for easier de-rigging. I couldn't see my crew on the road.

'Do you have me in sight yet? I am passing over Salt Flat at about 1500 feet.'

Then, I saw Boots standing in the spot where she wanted me to touch down. Even with the strong headwinds, the air was good, and I wanted every last bit of contest distance I could get.

'Hook'em up and come-a-running," I radioed, "I'm not throwing away 400 feet.'

"I could see Boots scurrying back to the car. I landed just short of the Salt Lake, at the west end of the bridge where I could go no further. I came in fifth for the day, but was not far behind the third and fourth place finishers. The next day was called for a rest day, and the fifth day was unflyable. So on Day six, we drove to Dallas where the Texas Soaring Association gliderport was the setting for another fine party. Another weather delay on Day six brought Dema (Lodema's namesake) and her husband up from Waco. Dema gave me a little stuffed pig and told me to carry it on the rest of the trip. With it, I was supposed to hog the rest of the days. It was my companion for the remainder of the race.

"On Day seven, we flew to Cimarron Airport (west of Oklahoma City) with relatively few problems, and I came in second for the day. On Day eight, and bound for Springfield, Missouri, I just beat out Paul Bikle for a first for the day. On Day nine, a heavy cirrus overcast was moving in over Springfield from the west, and it was getting heavier by the minute. We finally were instructed to 3,000-foot tows for timed releases, and, if we had to, we could land at a couple of airports ten to fifteen miles down the road. No one had ever yet flown over this country on any of the four previous Smirnoff Derbies, much less made it to the Mississippi River and St. Louis. What started out to be a very short distance day soon blossomed into the best day since the beginning of the Derby. I instructed Nan 6 to leave the interstate and come south to the highway leading to Cedar Hill, as landing near there appeared a certainty.

"I worked my way around the southern edge of St. Louis and was faced with a certain landing near the west bank of the Mississippi. As I flew over what appeared to be a prison along the water's edge, I knew that I must try to fly over. As I swung out over the river to set up my downwind leg, I hit a gust of a ridge lift from the tall trees among the river bank. I zoomed up and pointed the nose of the 1-35 across the river towards the east bank, figuring I had just enough altitude with 200 feet. Things went pretty well for a few seconds until I hit heavy down from the lee of the levy on the east bank. I was settling into the west bank when the air calmed and I serenely crossed over the trees, the levy, and landed just short of some high-tension lines. A Smirnoff pilot had finally flown across the Mississippi! It was a big deal for me. My 190 miles gave me another first and moved me into second place overall.

"On Day ten, we had rest and rain. The next day we trailered to Indianapolis, and on Day twelve, I moved into the overall lead. Day thirteen was another rest day full of games and movies. On our next flying day, Day fourteen into the race, we encountered lots of cold wind heading toward Latrobe, Pennsylvania. As I landed on a rocky plowed field nine miles short of Latrobe, Danny made it into Latrobe for the first completion of the Derby and gained many points on me. He was just one point behind me in second place overall heading into the last race day.

"In a discussion the next day waiting for the rain to clear, Danny admitted that his lucky number was one and that the night before his amazing flight to Latrobe, he had slept in a room with the number 111. As Boots and I checked into a hotel closer to Latrobe that night, the clerk handed me a key for room number 111. My lucky numbers tended to be 2s and 4s, which brought Boots to say, "Do you want that? Those are not our numbers." I told the clerk we would keep the room, reckoning that one first is not as good as three and besides it might shake Danny up a bit. We put a sign on the door that read, "MOJO lives on!"

"The next morning, Victory Day, there was still strong westerlies blowing, but clouds had started forming during the briefing. Danny had been flying superbly, and I would need all the speed points I could get to beat him. I released over the quarry at 3,000 feet and headed north over the ridge. Looking back, I saw that Danny had released and headed south toward better clouds. I got out of eyeshot as soon as possible and told Nan 6 to move out and hold near Latrobe. Watching the airport from afar, when the last glider was on tow I headed back. I worried that my plan might backfire because some heavy high cirrus was rapidly moving in from the west. I would have to make this fast. I landed with my water load still aboard. I didn't know for sure if I wanted other pilots to know I was making a re-light and re-start. I decided to keep my radio quiet, as the advantage of a later start should be all I would need – if I could escape the oncoming cloud cover. My tow pilot blew my cover because he headed west and just kept going, and I had to go on the air to direct him back to the quarry and then announce my release to Smirnoff Ground. I couldn't find good lift. Had I outsmarted myself?

"Oh well, this was do or don't, so I streaked out with 3,500 feet. Basically, the flight across the Alleghenies was uneventful. There were some anxious moments for all of us at times. Things were pretty choppy, but there were lots of good lift and waves that none of us bothered with. At one point, I got to base and 8,500 MSL and had plenty for a fast glide to the Derby finish line at Frederick, not counting the strong tailwind. The wide valley at Hagerstown was void of clouds, and was in a heavy sink. My reserve altitude came and went, but the ridge between Hagerstown and Frederick had a good cloud over it. I had heard Rudy and Bill call the finish gate a little earlier, so I knew they had made it, but decided to insure my flight with another 1,000 feet to take care of any sink on the lee side of the ridge. I had gained 400 feet when I heard Danny calling the gate. That did it. I stopped circling and gun sighted the 1-35's nose toward the airport. The extra 400 feet came in handy, but I arrived with no problems other than anxiety. On the way in, I could tell that Danny was still some distance out, so I relaxed a little. We had won. MOJO!

Suspended in Air and Space

In 1976 Boots, would yet again fly into the arms of her champion when Wally won his second Smirnoff Sailplane Derby. The day after the festivities where Wally was toasted and most likely roasted at the same time. The Nan 6 'MOJO' clan would pack up the sailplane and head back to Odessa. The trip from Frederick, Maryland to Odessa by car would take significantly less time than the way there. With no waiting on weather or retrieving the sailplane from a field, the trip home was rather uneventful.

Wally and Boots would return home to an empty house. Seree had recently re-married and had left Odessa for Hawkins, Texas. Wally Jr. was teaching in Midland and about to get married and living in Sherman, Texas. Dema and Deby remained close to one another in Waco, Texas, and both worked for the Waco Independent School District.

With Wally Jr.'s marriage, his relationship with his parents ceased. Wally Jr.'s new wife Lucinda felt that Wally and Boots did not approve of her. Because of this, Wally Jr. choose not to speak to his father for the 26 remaining years of his dad's life. This was especially difficult for Wally, who had depended on his son for crewing, flying, companionship and friendship. Wally and Boots would continue their attempts to see Wally Jr. and his children, but it would take over 25 years and the work of Wally Jr.'s eldest daughter, Molly, to finally bring the family back together in 2003. Boots would eventually develop a relationship with Wally Jr.'s children, but Wally Jr. and his father would not speak to each other again before Wally died. Wally would continue to focus on his flying and the rest of his family, but the toll the estrangement of Wally Jr. would take on the family was immense.

After returning to Odessa in the summer of 1976, Wally flew 540 miles to Bonny Dam, Idalia, Colorado, and won the Barringer award on August 18th. Wally would go on to win the Barringer for six out of the next seven straight years! His flight of 716.31 miles in 1977 broke his own record from 1971 and would also win him another National Record. He would once again win a National Record and the Barron Hilton Cup in 1985 for a 545.36-mile triangle flight. Wally would fly in the Smirnoff in 1977 and place third overall. The next year would be his last Smirnoff Derby, and he would place second. He would also continue to compete in the U.S. Nationals, always placing in the top ten in every event.

In 1978, the Smithsonian Museum in Washington, D.C. honored Wally by displaying at the National Air and Space Museum the Schweizer 1-35A, the sailplane he had flown to victory in the 1976 Smirnoff Derby. Always in good company, Wally's Schweizer 1-35A was placed suspended in soaring flight above a Sisu 1A, flown by fellow Odessan pilot Al Parker, who had set a world record in it. The two sailplanes would remain on display for two years and honored not only the pilots, but also America's best efforts in the fifteen-meter wingspan design class.

The prestige of having his sailplane in the Smithsonian supported Wally's view that gliding was 'One of America's fastest growing sports,' and indeed it was the efforts of the sailplane pioneer pilots that contributed to the growth of the sport in the '70s and '80s. Wally's picture still hangs in the National Air and Space Museum today.

The summers of the early '80s brought more long distance flights, National contests and records. In 1982, Wally won his first Barron Hilton Cup for a 533-mile flight on July 23th from Brownsville, TX to 5 miles south-east of Bowie, TX.

In December of 1985, at the age of 61, Wally would be recognized again. This time the recognition was received from the country of Chile. Guido Haymann and the Club de Planeadores de Santiago (the Glider

Club of Santiago) had long been intrigued by the soaring possibilities along the Andes mountain range. They had already discovered around 500-km of the stretch of the Cordillera de los Andes in their local flying, but they longed to know about the Cordillera's virtually unexplored regions. Thus, they decided to invite some of the World's best glider pilots to fly with them from Santiago to Arica, the northernmost city in Chile. Among the pilots invited to fly with the Chileans 1700-km (1056 miles) up the western flank of the Andes, were Wally Scott, Dick Schreder, Karl Striedieck, and Ed Byars from the US, Deither Memmert from Germany and Claude Calleja from France.

Attack on Aconcagua

Adapted from: Wallace Scott and Guido Haymann,
Soaring Magazine, May / June 1986

"It was a long time ago, and I was sitting on the edge of my seat, enthralled by what I was seeing on the screen. It was a Walt Disney color cartoon about flying. There was this family of cartoon airplanes, and the father was an old tri-motor type who flew the mail across the Andes. One day he came down sick, and there was no one to take the mail through but his young son, a boisterous single-engine monoplane with large, cute eyes and a tall rudder that continuously wagged to show the world how eager he was to please his old dad.

"Despite parental apprehension, the youngster shouldered the mailbag and took off in deteriorating weather, soon to be buffeted by storms as he approached the mountains. Blasts of icy wind sent him reeling end over end as he struggled to climb, gasping in the thin air. And then, through crashes of thunder and lightning, the dark clouds rolled apart and he was confronted with the fearsome and craggy visage of ACONCAGUA! Its awesome fissures and rocks looked like the true face of the earth's most vile and unforgiving bad guy. The little plane was terrified for an instant, and almost lost his mailbag, but he fought his way on.

"I'm sure this story ended with a happy ending. His story has stuck

189

with me since I was a young boy. When the opportunity to fly the Andes was given to me, I looked at some National Geographic magazines and some maps of Chile, and what was I to see near Santiago at the border of Argentina, but the old granddad, labeled for all to see…Aconcagua! At 22, 841 feet, the highest point in the entire American continent, he would be a challenge to reckon with. My turn was coming at last!

"Supported by the Chilean Air Force, LAN Chile, Shell Oil, Hotel Carrera, The Chilean Auto Club and Consorcio Neito Hermanos, our small brigade was off to fly the Andes. Boots accompanied me to Chile and on the trip down on January 5, 1986, LAN Chile Airlines treated us like royalty. Upon arrival in Chile, we were escorted to the a the VIP room where we were interviewed before taking a charter bus to Santiago's premiere hotel, the Carrera, for five nights of free accommodation and excellent service.

"The next day, we went to the Club de Planeadores de Santiago, a beautiful gliderport that I would like to have in West Texas. A flowing river bordering its southern edge, eucalyptus trees 125 feet tall bordering the northern edge, and a single paved east-west runway created the most serene gliderport I've ever seen. While up on my check flight that afternoon, I began feeling sick and had to come down. The problem was to plague me for some time. On January 8, the pilots all met for a recon flight in the Chilean Air Force Twin Otter over the entire route to Arica. On this flight, we found that not only were there no thermals in the air, the land below was completely unlandable, and I mean completely.

"I was still feeling sick on January 9 and started taking pills for an apparent stomach bug I had picked up. I wanted to get well quick or at least hold everything together in limbo. Our exploration was to start in two days, and I didn't want to get shot out of the saddle now. On our first expedition day, I flew in one of three Januses with Guido Haymann. The first leg was from Santiago to Vicuna. With full survival gear for two, plus ten gallons of water in the wings that we would never dump and drinking water in the cockpit, we were off. We had worked out an agreement that the person off the controls had a main job to keep track of navigation, as well as watching ahead for decision points. Guido kept on track and was full of advice on decisions….up to a point. Once we passed the point of his furthest excursions from Santiago, the back seat became very quiet. Unknown vistas lay ahead for both of us.

"The higher elevations were cloud covered, and our attained altitudes were about 3,000 to 3,500 meters (9,800 to 11,500 ft). But, a feeling of anomaly began to set in for me: what worked over our western deserts and mountains was not working here. Except on rare occasions, if you headed for a good cumulus cloud a few miles ahead, the lift would long be gone by the time you could get there. It soon became quite clear that the flight would have to be supported by the pure orographic lift generated from wind flowing over the mountains.

"We did find one or two good thermals upwind from well-configured terrain, and a cu would start forming overhead, but it would dissipate long before we could get to cloud base. Flying the ridges very closely, we often would make turns in up shafts of air that would net nothing but a scare. Cruising near the tops of some of the ridges, I would receive a heavy push under my ridge-side wing, only to turn into the sink generated by a very narrow band of lift and wind, being able to escape only with a net loss of altitude.

"Another anomaly was that the lift would seldom take us beyond ridge height, not at all like cruising down the western Rocky Mountains at 18,000 or 20,000 feet, following long cloud streets that would be productive for hours on end. At thirty-five miles out, with no thermals to be expected, and only 4,300 feet above our destination airport elevation, I turned the controls over to Guido to integrate some of his expertise. I warned him not to lose any more altitude.

'Where is the airport?' he asked.

"I told him to stay with the ridge, as it ran directly into the airport. At last, we arrived at 4,300 feet. He had done it again. I offered my congratulations, and he proceeded to chew me out and tell me how lucky I was, 'We just don't do those things!' he said referring to ridge flying. On the flight out of Vicuna to the mining town of El Salvador three days later, we chose the wrong ridge and ended up landing out at Vallenar airport. We had to be towed to El Salvador with two other Januses.

"The Chileans had voiced disappointment that the Americans didn't do enough reporting by radio. So, once or twice Schreder called me to find out how we were doing. 'Fine,' I would tell him. When we finally caught up with him, after about an hour, I asked him how it was going for him. 'OK,' was his reply. This type of exchange was driving the Chilean pilots mad, as they were continually reporting positions and conditions to their fellow pilots. We never heard from Karl, and I'm sure he flew with his radio off most of the time. I would have liked to turn ours off, and would turn the volume down to an acceptable level, only to have Guido demand that I turn up the volume.

"January 13th was a day of rest, and as the Chileans were concerned about flying out of El Salvador, a meeting was held to discuss the issue. The Chileans are, of necessity, primarily ridge pilots and rock polishers. The mountains along this part of the Cordillera Domeyko are not conducive to ridge flying, having slow and gradual elevation changes. This, plus the thirty-to-fifty miles walking distance to civilization, warranted much concern. In the end, some were towed to a dirt strip part way along the next leg to try it from there, but we opted to trailer the Janus to Calama.

"On a day of local flying, before we launched our 'Attack on Aconcagua,' or more correctly, 'Attempt on Aconcagua,' Guido and I were working thermals upwind of the airport. Guido became disgruntled saying, 'Why do you always circle to the right?'

I replied, 'If my right wing kicks up, I turn to the right.'

'But why don't you turn left?' he demanded.

'If you want to turn left, *you* fly it,' I shot back.

He took the controls, flew a few miles, and hit a thermal. He turned to the right!

'Why in hell are you turning right?' I asked.

'Damned if I know!' he replied.

We both laughed our heads off. We flew for about four hours and came in to prepare for our attack.

"Never have I ever been so concerned about a 150-mile flight. The fact that the terrain we were about to cover had never been flown before was only part of what concerned me; the weather patterns that allowed for part of the Atacama Desert to never have recorded rainfall meant that thermals in the area were probably scarce as well.

"On January 16th, on our route from Calama to the coastal city of Iquique, Guido and I towed into the central plain to see whether it would work, but stayed close to the Pan American Highway for good landing sites. After we released fifty-five km (34 miles) northwest of Calama, we found relatively good thermals, lift and little wind. I felt right at home, and we made good time for about fifty km until conditions worsened. When we could get no more than 1200 meters (4,000 ft) above the ground and had thirty-five km (22 miles) to go to the next landable site, we began focusing our attention solely on making it to ground safely. Things weren't looking good; Alex Chanes radioed that he would have to land on the road. About now, Mike Lambie, the ex-military pilot, radioed from the L-19 that there seemed to be a landable piece of road about fourteen miles ahead.

"With nowhere else to go we headed for it, very low and nursing every scrap of lift and patch of zero sink. We got there with a spare 100 feet or so, enough to make a fly-by and look it over. 'Guido,' I said, 'we will have to make it over the electric lines, and there is a large pile of debris we will have to clear. There is another pile a little further on, but it is smaller, and our wings will clear it. We will touch down there.' It was barely possible. Guido asked if I wanted the drag chute; I told him to put his hand on the release and be ready to deploy it fast, but only if I called for it. There were some large rocks scattered about, but there seemed to be an avenue between them. We cleared the wires and the large pile of debris, and I told him the chute would not be needed. We touched down alongside the low pile, rolled a few yards, and I was able to let the wing down between the rocks on soft

193

sand. 'Beautiful!' said Guido. 'Whew!' I said, not wanting to have to do that again to prove it.

"We had about a four-hour wait on the desert until the tow plane arrived to take us on to Iquique. When Mike arrived in the L-19, he asked for Guido to take the front seat, and I was planning to hook us up. But, just in time Alex Chanes and his ground crew drove up on the way back after their retrieve, and I hopped in back as we now had a wing-runner. As soon as we took off, I was glad for our successful outlanding, as the terrain everywhere around was terrible: large areas of solid rock and moonscape. With about thirty miles to go and mountains poking up through the clouds, the radio came alive in Spanish, and Mike told Guido to use the dive brakes. Even so, our descent speeds were reaching well into the yellow speed arc. We crossed mountains and below clouds with just scant feet in between, and Mike flew down valleys beneath lowering ceilings to stay out of the clouds. I thanked heaven for half-inch Nylon towropes. We finally landed at Iquique with the last light of the day.

"It was slowly becoming apparent that soaring in the Atacama Desert would not be quite possible, and the motor plane would have to tow us to Arica. The last leg of the rally on January 17th would be smooth behind the power of the tow plane and, even then, we kept close to the coast. Striedieck decided to fly the coastal ridges, he made it using power only at the beginning. Radic was towed to about 3,500 meters (11,000 feet). He managed to use the ridge lift and thermaled under the cumulus where the ridge-lift conditions were poor, but he managed to make it to the airport of Arica. Only Striedieck and Radic made the flight without much use of the tow plane, but when the entire gang was received at the airport, it was as if we all had. There was a press conference the following day where everyone received official honors. The next two days were spent touring the city and its surroundings, putting the gliders together, and resting.

"On January 24, with Guido rested from a trip back south, we declared AA day: Attack on Aconcagua. We were finally going to attempt it, and we tried hard, very hard, and got close. Just a scant couple of miles short, but we couldn't get over or beyond his lower teeth. We even went places Guido advised against, and saw a lot more formidable terrain and got jolted around somewhat, but the old granddad won this day. We would have to try again tomorrow. On the 25th, we tried again with the forecast much better. Winds were forecast to be straight out of the west and increasing with altitude. We hit good solid thermals just beyond the first ridge, and our hopes soared. Srdjan Radic had declared a 1,000-km (622 miles) flight and taken off at nine a.m. As we worked our first thermal, he joined us. Being a little behind in his time, he would abort his triangle and join us in our assault. Two other gliders soon joined us, and away we went.

"Everything went great for a while, good lift over the ridges and seemingly pure thermals. Then we hit one ridge that had given us no trouble before, and spent thirty minutes trying to top it. We never did, but we got close. Radic and the others were ahead, reporting problems. We finally arrived at the lower teeth of Aconcagua, and tightened our seat belts. But…from this point on, the reader will have to guess at the outcome. The gentleman or the tiger? I know. Guido knows. The Chileans all know. And, yes, the mountain knows too.[5]

Flying back to the strip, I was enjoying myself. The last two days, I think the bug had finally gone. Guido was enjoying the flying, also swooping and pushing rocks (almost) and screeching up and over sharp ridges and diving into steep canyons. 'You know, Wally,' Guido said, 'you really scared me the way you flew the ridges at first. 'You know, Guido,' I replied, 'you scared me too, at first!' I will come to the end of our flying with this observation: If Guido is number ten on their list of pilots who fly close to the ridges, I do not think I want to fly with numbers one through nine.

---

[5] Note: According to Boots, Wally and Guido did make it to the top of Acongacua mountain.

Go Like Hell

Wally and Boots returned from the Andes with an experience and a half under their belts. Wally would continue to fly locally right through the summer following the trip, attended the Barron Hilton Cup in July 1986, and finished the summer winning the Barringer trophy for his 526.6-mile flight on August 13, 1986. He would win the Barringer trophy five more times in 1987, 1988, 1989, 1990 and 1993 for a total of twenty Barringer wins.

Contest flying remained second fiddle to Wally's distance flying, but a trip towards Refugio that brought him to a small town called Uvalde, Texas, brought him back to the contest front. Red Wright had retired to his ranch at Leakey near Uvalde, and another friend, Ron Tabery was currently based out of the Uvalde airport. With good people, aero tows readily available, plenty of tiedown spaces and great flying conditions, Uvalde seemed too good to be true. Becoming enchanted, Boots and Wally made fast friends with new glider pilot and Uvalde FBO owner Mark Huffstutler, who was under the tutelage of Ron Tabery. A quick learner and a talented pilot, Mark enjoyed the company of the seasoned teacher, a relationship that would develop into a lifelong friendship.

Leading into the last day and ultimately coming in sixth at the 55th Open Class National Soaring Championships held in Uvalde in August of 1988, Wally always managed to put on a good show while flying contests, even though his heart belonged to distance. One of the most underrated contest pilots, according to pilot Sherman Griffith, Wally was always near the top in every contest he participated in.

The morning of Wally's longest recorded flight started out just as any other. On July 14, 1995, the weather looked right, and the cumulus clouds were forming early. So, Boots and Wally headed to the airport. Once Wally was up in the air, Boots started driving after him, staying on the road until she was past Seminole, Texas. At this point, she lost both radio and phone connection and wasn't quite sure where he was or where he was headed. So, she started back toward Odessa. Once she was home, she turned on the radio and eventually heard him calling in as he headed back toward Odessa from the Oklahoma panhandle. Boots quickly hopped in the car and was at the airport when he landed. Thinking he wasn't going to make it back, much less that this would be his longest flight ever, Wally was thrilled. The flight would be a total of 808 miles! Unfortunately, since Wally had declared a straight-out distance flight and ended up making an out-and-return flight, it did not win him the Barringer. It would, however, put him within an astonishing 192 miles of his ultimate goal to reach 1,000 miles.

For the next few years, Wally flew mostly locally until January 7, 1999, when he underwent knee surgery. With seventy-four years under his belt, Wally faced a critical challenge. This knee surgery, though routine, would mark the beginning of the end of his soaring career. The surgery not only weakened his body, but, unable to climb into his sailplane, it also weakened his spirit. A few months after the surgery, Boots took Wally to the airport to visit and wash his pride and joy ASW-20 and assess the extent of the damage to his body. With some help from Boots, Wally was able to enter his home away from home: the cockpit of the ASW-20. Sitting in the cockpit, Wally attempted to go through his regular routine of preparing for a flight when he simply looked up at Boots with tearful eyes and said, 'I don't think I can do this anymore. I can't understand what the instruments are telling me.'

Whether it was the oncoming stages of Alzheimer's or the realization that he would never again be able to fly as he used to, Wally knew that his life in a sailplane had come to an end. Shortly after knee-surgery, Wally was diagnosed with Alzheimer's and Boots stayed right by his side for the remaining four and a half years of his life. Always right together, depending on each other for life itself, Boots and Wally would find peace in their daily routine of coffee and prayer in the mornings on the back porch. On a rare day, when Boots would leave the house to run errands and a friend would come to be with Wally, he would stand by the door waiting for his wife to return.

During this time, Deby's husband James became terminally ill, and Boots and Wally made daily trips to their daughter's house to water plants and keep up the house. Wally would go with Boots for company, but, unable to do any yard work, he would sit in the carport with Deby's small dog Sable. By the time James and Deby returned home for their last months together, Wally had become attached to Sable. When Boots and Wally went to welcome them home, Wally again sat with Sable for most of the afternoon. He then walked up to Deby and said, 'I want this dog.'

Sable was with him from then on. Always providing good company, Sable would sit on Wally's lap throughout most of his final days. On the night before Wally went into hospice care, he called out to Boots, who put her arms around him, telling him how much she loved him. Unable to speak coherently by this point, Wally simply muttered to his wife, who knew exactly what he was saying. Boots recalled, 'We always thought we had forever. We were looking forward to flying until the end.'

Ultimately it would be pneumonia that would take Boots' Wallace from her on February 8, 2003. The funeral, held at Schleymeyer Airport in Odessa, included three gliders and two power planes flying overhead in the 'missing man' formation. The power planes buzzed the hangar followed by the gliders, then two gliders made a turn to the right and the third kept going straight. Gary Evans, a friend and mentee of Wally's, dropped the ashes. They were spread first over Radcliffe Stadium, home to Wally's famed MOJO football passion, and then over Schleymeyer Airport. The United States Air Force presented three flags—one to each daughter. Unable to procure a fourth, Boots' grandson Cody promised to get Boots a flag that flew over Burma to honor Wally being stationed there during the war.

'He was a John Wayne type of a guy,' gliding friend Sherman Griffith remembers. 'When you think about strong personalities and people you remember from our sport, I think about Fritz Kahl, Red Wright and Wally. He was single-minded, he had a dream, and he just kept chipping away at it.' After a total of 6,624.5 logged hours and 303,142 miles of cross-country ultimately conquered, Wally's lifetime of soaring had come to an end. He would hold a total of four World Records at one point or another in his lifetime and after. After Wally passed away, he would win the Joseph C. Lincoln writing award from Soaring Magazine for his article on the preparation and execution of long distance flights on February 8, 2004. Wally's life as one of the world's best soaring pilots in the world was commemorated with an exhibits in both the Odessa Museum and in the Texas Aviation Hall of Fame in Galveston. 'He was bigger than life,' Jim Callaway says. 'There will never be anyone like him again.' Wally's passion and commitment to soaring, every day for the greater part of his life, remains an inspiration to all those who knew him and all those who will remember his soaring legacy.

For Boots, she had lost her other half, which she had a hard time dealing with at first. As Wally would often ask in his final years, 'Why did this happen to me?' Boots now found she was asking herself the same question. Over the next few years, Boots continued to find strength in the love and memory of her life with Wallace Scott, the hours of flying, of living and loving with their children and two entirely full lives lived in one. Boots imagines that Wally is still chasing that 1,000-mile flight, hunting for early morning cumulus clouds from the top of a roof, always going for more distance, staying consistently passionate and true to his soaring and to his wife, forever plus two days.

Appendix

	Date	Accomplishment	Flight Notes
1961	April 2nd	FAI Silver Badge for Altitude – 1500 meters above low point	Odessa, blue thermals, wind 20 mph, 73°F, westerly winds and clear skies
	April 3rd	FAI Silver Badge for Distance attempt – 39 miles	From Odessa, TX to Monahans, TX and return. Rejected – no barograph on board
	April 15th	FAI Silver Badge for Distance – 35.5 miles	From Odessa, TX to Crane, TX. Blue thermals, 65°F
	May 25th	FAI Silver 'C' Duration 120 miles – 5-hour Duration Badge #481	From Odessa, TX to Big Spring to Sterling City to Barnhart to Mertzon to Tankersley, TX
	August 18th	78 miles	From Odessa, TX to Wellman, TX
	August 27th	122 miles	From Odessa, TX to Morton, TX
	August 28th	177 miles	From Odessa, TX to Bovina, TX
	September 1st	FAI Gold Badge for Altitude – 4,000 meters	Odessa, TX, blue thermals
	September 2nd	182 miles	From Odessa, TX to Haskell, TX, 46 mph
1962	June 16	FAI Gold Badge for Goal Distance – 186 miles	From Odessa, TX to Hereford, TX, low point 400 ft (to declared goal)
	August 12th	FAI Gold Badge for Distance – 330 miles	From Odessa, TX to Plains, TX to Roswell, NM to Tucumcari, NM (declared dog leg distance) Good Conditions, Low Point 500ft

	Date	Accomplishment	Flight Notes
1963	August 6th	Distance Record for 1-26 - 443.5 miles	From Odessa, TX to Lovington, NM to Clayton, NM
1964	June 29th – July 9th	31st U.S. National Soaring Championships – 2nd Place Overall	1st glider contest, McCook, NE Ka-6 CR
	July 23rd	FAI World Record – Straight distance to a declared goal 520.55 miles / 837.75km	From Odessa, TX to Goodland, KS Ka-6 CR
1965	May 2nd	FAI Diamond Badge # 42 for Altitude – 5,486 meters	Odessa, TX
	May 20th – June 11th	10th World Gliding Championships – 6th Place Finish, Standard Class	South Cerney, England, Ka-6 CR
	June 28th	32nd U.S. National Soaring Championships – 10th Place Overall	3rd Contest Adrian, Michigan
1966	June 25th	33rd U.S. National Soaring Championships – 16th Place Overall –	Reno, Nevada Ka-6 E
	July 28th	State Record 62 MPH	From Odessa, TX to Snyder to San Angelo, TX. 310 Mile Triangle
1967	July 4th – 14th	34th U.S. National Soaring Championships – 12th Place Overall	Marfa, TX
	August 23rd	Barringer Trophy– 552 miles	From Odessa, TX to Casa Grande, AZ
1968	July 19th – 25th	Marfa Regional – 6th Place Finish	

	Date	Accomplishment	Flight Notes
	August 5th	Barringer Trophy – 492.2 miles	From Odessa, TX to Oakley, KS
1969	June 24th – July 3rd	Marfa Nationals – 2nd Place Finish	ASW-12
	July 16th	452 miles	From Odessa, TX to Pratt, KS
	August 22nd	Barringer Trophy and FAI World Record Straight Distance to a declared Goal 605.23 miles / 974.04 km	From Odessa, TX to Gila Bend, AZ ASW-12
1970	June 22nd – July 3rd	FAI 12th World Gliding Championships, Marfa, TX – 9th Place overall	From Marfa, TX to Van Horn to Sierra Blanca and return (twice) 442 miles From Marfa, TX to Odessa, Big Lake, Wink, Sierra Blance and return – 482 miles ASW-12
	July 26	Barringer Trophy shared with Ben Greene, National and FAI World Free Distance Record – 716.95 miles / 1153.82 km FAI 1000 K Diploma #3	From Odessa, TX to Columbus, NE ASW-12
	August 3rd	FAI Out-and-return Distance Record –	From Odessa, TX to Pampas, TX and return

	Date	Accomplishment	Flight Notes
1971	July 2 th	534 miles / 860 km	ASW-12
		15-M National Record Odessa, TX PrimRose, NE 716.31 miles /	
	Sept 11th	Barringer Trophy– 578.48 miles	From Odessa, TX to Estrella, AZ
1972	May 1st – May 19th	1st Smirnoff Sailplane Derby – 1st Place Finish	
1973	May 1st – May 30th	2nd Smirnoff Sailplane Derby – 3rd Place Finish	
	July 21st – August 2nd	Nationals at Liberal Kansas – 4th Place Finish 642.09 miles	
1974	March 12th		Heart Attack
1975	July 15th	42nd U.S. National Soaring Championships – 3rd Place Overall	Hobbs, New Mexico ASW-12
	August 20th	Barringer Trophy– 600.9 miles	From Odessa, TX to Imperial, NE
1976	May 2nd – 22nd	5th Smirnoff Sailplane Derby – 1st Place Finish	Start in Los Angeles, CA. Finish in Frederick, Maryland.
	July 12th – 23rd	Standard Class Nationals – 14th Place Finish	Hutchinson, Kansas
	August 18th	Barringer Trophy – Standard Class Record – 540 miles	From Odessa, TX to Bonny Dam, Idalia, CO

	Date	Accomplishment	Flight Notes
1977	May 1st – 17th	6th Smirnoff Sailplane Derby – 3rd Place	
	July 2nd	Barringer Trophy and National Record – 716.31 miles	From Odessa, TX to Primrose, NE
	July 10th – 21st	Hobbs National Contest – 5th Place Overall	Hobbs, New Mexico 1-35A
1978	May 2nd – 21st	7th Smirnoff Sailplane Derby – 2nd Place Finish	Last Derby
	July 11th	590 miles	From Odessa, TX to Trenton, NE
	August 21st	Barringer Trophy - 628.98 miles	From Odessa, TX to Grant, NE
	September 6th	530 miles	From Odessa, TX to Salida, CO
	September 10th	580 miles	From Odessa, TX to Wray, CO
1979	July 14th – 26th	Standard Class Nationals 6th Place	Hutchinson, Kansas
	August 16th	Barringer Trophy – 590 miles	From Odessa, TX to McCook, NE
1980	June 11th – 26th	15-Meter Nationals - 4th Place Finish	Springfield, Ohio
	July 11th	Triangle Record 15-meter class 490.5 miles, 65.84 mph	From Odessa, TX to Roswell to Plainview, TX and return.

	Date	Accomplishment	Flight Notes
	July 13th – 24th	Open Class Nationals – 10th Place Finish	Hobbs, New Mexico
	August 9th	Barringer Trophy – 675 miles	From Odessa, TX to Stapleton, NE
1981	July 10th	637 miles	From Odessa, TX to Kearney, NE *lost the Barringer to Marion Griffith by 8.61 Miles
	July 13th – 23rd	Standard Class Nationals – 8th Place Finish	Hobbs, New Mexico
1982	July 23rd	Barringer Trophy – shared with William H. Seed Jr. 533 miles & qualifying WA for Barron Hilton Cup	From Brownsville, TX to 5 miles SE Bowie, TX
	August 27th	New National 15-meter class triangle record 79 MPH	From Odessa, TX to Snyder to San Angelo and return 315 XC Miles, 3hr 59min
	August 28th	425 miles	From Odessa, TX to Garden City, KS forced to land due to rain
1983	June 3rd	Open Class Nationals – 2nd Place Finish	Marana, Arizona
	July	Attending Barron Hilton Cup	Flying M. Ranch
	August 12th	655 miles, 8 hour flight	From Odessa, TX to Kimball Airport, NE

	Date	Accomplishment	Flight Notes
	August 17th	Barringer Trophy – 668.36 miles	From Odessa, TX to 3 miles north of Dalton, NE
	October 1st	622 miles, 7 hours 35 minutes	From Odessa, TX to 7 miles south of Haxtun, CO
1984	May 26th – June 12th	Littlefield TX Regional, 1st Place Finish	
	August 16th – 24th	Uvalde, TX Regional, 1st Place Finish	
	July 16th – 26th	Standard Class Nationals, 14th Place Finish	Hutchinson, Kansas
1985	July 1st – 11th	Hobbs Nationals, 5th Place Finish	
	August 31st	New Distance 15-meter class National Record, 545 miles – 68mph. Qualifying WA for Barron Hilton Cup	Wink and Return from Odessa, TX to Robert Lee to Del Rio. ASW-20
	August 4th – 22nd	Uvalde Regional, 1st Place Finish	
1986	January 7th – 25th	Flew Andes, Santiago to Arica at the Peruvian Border	Santiago, Chile
	July 19th-	Attended Barron Hilton Cup	Flying M. Ranch
	August 13th	Barringer Trophy 526.6 miles, 8 hour flight	Batesville to Perryton, Texas

	Date	Accomplishment	Flight Notes
1987	July 22nd	545 miles, 8 hour flight	From Odessa, TX to Goodland, KS
	August 25th	Barringer Trophy, 569.03 miles	From Uvalde, TX to Medicine Lodge, KS
1988	June 17th	418 miles	From Odessa, TX to Hobbs, TX to Tatum-Portales, NM and return
	June 18th	436 miles	From Odessa, TX to Hobbs, TX to Lamesa to Big Springs to Odessa to Rankin and return
	July 5th	Barringer Trophy, 716.74 miles	From Odessa, TX to Hyannis, NE *3rd 700 mile flight into Nebraska
	August 8th – 17th	Uvalde Nationals Open Class, 5th Place Finish	
	August 21st	638 miles	From Uvalde, TX to Larned, KS *1st 1000 KM flight from Uvalde
1989	July 11th	404 miles	From Odessa, TX to Johnson City, KS *cut off by cold front
	July 29th	Barringer Trophy, 649.16 miles	From Uvalde, TX to Great Bend, KS, *2nd 1000 KM flight from Uvalde
	August 31st	480 miles	From Odessa, TX to Harper, KS
1990	July 7th	Barringer Trophy 725.89 miles	From Odessa, TX to Thedford, NE
1991			*bad weather, only local and Uvalde flying

	Date	Accomplishment	Flight Notes
1992			* bad weather only local and Uvalde flying
1993	August 13th	440 miles	From Odessa, TX to Syracuse, KS
	August 17th	524 miles	From Odessa, TX to Burlington, CO
	Sept 21st	Barringer Trophy, 539.87 miles	From Odessa, TX to Goodland, KS
1994	August 27th	524 miles	From Odessa, TX to Oklahoma panhandle
1995	July 14th	Out-and-return 808 miles	From Odessa to Oklahoma panhandle *** WA longest flight
1997	July 24th	545 miles	From Odessa, TX to Goodland, KS

Lifetime flying totals: 6,624.25 hours and 303,142 miles flown in a glider

- FAI Silver Badges – Altitude gain of at least 1,000 meters. Distance straight line cross country of at least 31 miles. Duration of at least 5 hours in flight.
- FAI Gold Badges – Altitude gain of at least 3,000 meters. Distance straight line cross country of at least 186 miles. Duration of at least 5 hours in flight (only one has to be done to count for both silver and gold)
- FAI Diamond Badges – Altitude gain of at least 5,000 meters. Distance straight line cross country to a pre-determined goal of at least 186 miles and a distance of 310 miles (not necessarily to a pre-defined goal)

Awards and Recognition

1965	National Soaring Hall of Fame
1967	The Lewin B. Barringer Memorial Trophy: 552 mi.
1968	The Lewin B. Barringer Memorial Trophy: 492.2 mi
1969	The Lewin B. Barringer Memorial Trophy: 605.23 mi.
	Larissa Stroukoff Memorial Trophy
1970	The Lewin B. Barringer Memorial Trophy shared with Benjamin W. Greene: 716.952 mi.
	SSA Exceptional Achievement Award
1971	The Lewin B. Barringer Memorial Trophy: 578.48 mi.
1973	The Lewin B. Barringer Memorial Trophy: 642.09 mi.
1975	The Lewin B. Barringer Memorial Trophy: 600.9 mi.
1976	The Lewin B. Barringer Memorial Trophy: 540 mi.
1977	The Lewin B. Barringer Memorial Trophy: 716 mi.
1978	The Lewin B. Barringer Memorial Trophy: 628.98 mi.
1979	The Lewin B. Barringer Memorial Trophy: 590 mi.
1980	The Lewin B. Barringer Memorial Trophy: 675 mi
1982	The Lewin B. Barringer Memorial Trophy shared with William H. Seed Jr. 533 mi
	Barron Hilton Cup

1983	The Lewin B. Barringer Memorial Trophy: 668.36 mi
1985	Barron Hilton Cup
1986	The Lewin B. Barringer Memorial Trophy: 526.6 mi
1987	The Lewin B. Barringer Memorial Trophy: 569.03 mi
1988	The Lewin B. Barringer Memorial Trophy: 716.74 mi
	SSA Exceptional Achievement Award
1989	The Lewin B. Barringer Memorial Trophy: 649.16 mi
1990	The Lewin B. Barringer Memorial Trophy: 725.89 mi
1993	The Lewin B. Barringer Memorial Trophy: 539.87 mi
2004	Joseph C. Lincoln Writing Award 2004 – Soaring Magazine 2004 reprint from 1982 of an article titled "The Preparation and Execution of Long-Distance Flights."
2005	Inducted in Texas Aviation Hall of Fame

National Aeronautic Association and Federation Aeronautique Internationale (FAI) Awards

July 23, 1964	FAI World Record - Straight Distance to a declared goal: Odessa, TX – Goodland, KS 837.75 KM – Ka-6CR (N1304S) FAI record # 4406
July 12, 1965	10th FAI World Soaring Championship, South Cherney, England 6th place overall
August 22, 1969	FAI World Record – Straight Distance to a declared goal: Odessa, TX – Gila Bend, AZ. 974.04 KM – ASW 12 (N134Z) FAI record # 4408
July 26, 1970	FAI World Record – Straight Distance Odessa, TX – Columbus, NE 1,153.821 KM – ASW 12 (N4472) FAI record # 5409
August 3, 1970	FAI World Record – Out-and-Return Odessa, TX – Pampas, TX and return 860.00 KM – ASW 12 (N4472) FAI record # 5421
July 4, 1970	12th FAI World Gliding Championship, Marfa, TX. 9th place overall

July 2, 1977	15-M National Record Odessa, TX – Primrose, NE 716.31 miles /1152.79 KM
July 11, 1980	15-M Triangle Record Odessa, TX – Roswell, NM, Plain View, TX & return 750 KM / 7hrs 27min / 65.84mph
August 31, 1985	545 mile Triangle – 15-M Record Odessa, TX – Robert Lee, TX, Del Rio ,TX Wink, TX 68 mph Also qualified for Barron Hilton Cup winning flight

The Smirnoff Sailplane Derby

1972 – 1st Smirnoff Sailplane Derby	1st Place Finish
1973 – 2nd Smirnoff Sailplane Derby	3rd Place Finish
1974 – 3rd Smirnoff Sailplane Derby	*had heart attack March 12, 1974 did not fly
1975 – 4th Smirnoff Sailplane Derby	*did not fly
1976 – 5th Smirnoff Sailplane Derby	1st Place Finish
1977 – 6th Smirnoff Sailplane Derby	3rd Place Finish
1978 – 7th Smirnoff Sailplane Derby	2nd Place Finish

Notes

In 1978 he made three long flights in 14 days:
1: Odessa to Grant, Nebraska – 630 miles
2: Odessa to Salida, Colorado – 530 miles
3: Odessa to Wray, Colorado – 580 miles

World War II Experience:

During World War II he flew 126,000 miles, this includes his time at Fort Stockton, Texas. He was commissioned June 3, 1944 at Nashville, Tennessee. Air Transport Command. He became Air Force Military Airlines, First Officer. Operations officer at Dum Dum, instrument check pilot, route check pilot, instrument green card holder, staff first pilot.

He was in Ardennes, Central Europe and Central Burma, and flew many missions during the Battle of the Bulge. He received the American Theater Ribbon, EAME Theatre Ribbon with 2 bronze stars, Air Medal, World War II Victory Medal and a commendation from his base commander.

Proficient in the following aircrafts: Piper J2, J3, J4, J5 Cub, Taylor Craft, Culver Cadet, PT 17, PT 19, BT 13, AT6, AT11, C45, C46, C47, B17, B24, B25, A20.

Boots Scott, recipient of the 1991 SSA Exceptional Achievement Award, at Wallace's desk at home in Odessa, TX 2010. She is holding her husband's Texas Aviation Hall of Fame Trophy and Medal.

Acknowledgements

First and foremost, this book was written for Boots Scott and it was because of Boots that this book came to fruition. Without her undying support and patience this tribute to Wally would not have been possible. I thank Boots with all of my heart for allowing me to become a part of her family and finish what Wally began.

Thank you to Mark Huffstutler for seeing this project through to the end, from the simple 'summer project' start to the ultimate finish and for lending his technical expertise to a very needy manuscript. I would especially like to thank Karin Schlösser and BT Link Publishing for taking over just in time and seeing that this manuscript made it to print. I am eternally grateful for your help and knowledge of the gliding community.

I would like to note that though the relationship between Wally and his son Wally Jr. was not resolved before Wally's death, Wally Jr. has since reconciled with Boots and the rest of the Scott family and now visits and maintains weekly communication with his mother. I would sincerely like to thank Wally Jr. for his help in reviewing the manuscript and aiding with some of the more personal details of the storyline.

For their technical guidance and patience with endless questions, thank you to Sherman Griffith, Marion Griffith and James Callaway. To my editor Liana Orshan for being my saving grace in the final attempt to finish the manuscript, thank you for being so efficient. Thank you to Soaring Magazine for allowing me the use of Wallace Scott's articles. Thank you to the Soaring Society of America and in particular to Denise Layton.

Special thanks goes to Tufts University and my writing advisor Michael Ullman for allowing me to take this book as an English Class. To Katie Gadkowski for lending her photographic skills, to Laura Lee Timko for her publishing expertise and everyone else who read pages of the manuscript.

Most importantly thank you to my mother, Kim Fulton, for everyday encouragement and reading draft upon draft when I know reading is not usually something she enjoys. Thank you for staying on me and standing by me always.

Lastly, to my husband Charlie for constant support and encouragement in what was mostly, for the better part of a decade, a big stack of papers.

Samantha Hilbert Thomas is an Associate Producer for NBC Sports and won an Emmy for her work on the NBC coverage of the Beijing Olympics. A graduate of Tufts University, she lives in New York City with her husband Charlie Thomas. **WA** – *the life of soaring legend Wally Scott* is her first book.

Breinigsville, PA USA
27 January 2011
254281BV00003B/2/P

9 780983 130604